DOLLS &
DOLL HOUSES

by Flora Gill Jacobs
& Estrid Faurholt

Frontispiece: The Interior of the Tiffany House (See *Color Plate 8*)

A Book of

DOLLS

&

DOLL HOUSES

by Flora Gill Jacobs
and
Estrid Faurholt

CHARLES E. TUTTLE COMPANY
RUTLAND, VERMONT & TOKYO, JAPAN

Representatives:
For Continental Europe: BOXER BOOKS INC, Zurich

For the British Isles: PRENTICE-HALL INTERNATIONAL, INC., London

For Australasia: PAUL FLESCH & CO., PTY. LTD., Melbourne

Published by:
THE CHARLES E. TUTTLE COMPANY, INC.
of Rutland, Vermont & Tokyo, Japan
with editorial offices at Suido 1-chōme, 2-6, Bunkyo-ku, Tokyo

Library of Congress Catalog No. 65-20615

[PRINTED IN JAPAN]
THE VOYAGERS' PRESS, TOKYO

FOREWORD

AT A TIME WHEN MORE AND MORE DOLL COLLECTORS ARE *beginning to include doll houses in their collections, it seems especially appropriate to give a few words of introduction to the first book written exclusively about dolls and doll houses.*

Although there have, of course, been many books about dolls, there have been relatively few about doll houses. A History of Dolls' Houses[1] and English Dolls' Houses of the Eighteenth and Nineteenth Centuries[2], the two comprehensive studies, were preceded by a volume about Dutch doll houses at the turn of the century, the handsome two-volume set about Queen Mary's doll house in 1924, and a few booklets printed by museums in between.

This volume was begun with the notion of combining dolls and their residences, two topics similar but divergent. It is true that most doll houses of consequence are inhabited by dolls—by very small dolls, however, which are only a minor branch of doll collecting. Most of the dolls sought by doll collectors are too sizeable to take advantage of the comforts and conveniences which might be theirs if only they might wedge a small foot inside a still smaller door. It is presumed that many collectors of dolls are primarily interested in costume, while most collectors of doll houses are embroiled in a gamut of preoccupations ranging from the furnishings through the customs of the past.

Innumerable museum dolls have been pictured, some of them repeatedly, in one volume or another; usually prints are available and republication is uncomplicated. At a time when old dolls and doll houses, like all antiques, are becoming increasingly difficult to find, a time when the treasure discovered in an attic must be less romantically replaced by the treasure bought at the sombre breaking-up of a collection, it seemed to us that a book about dolls and doll houses, mostly those of the nineteenth century, still available to collectors would be a useful and attractive guide. We have also undertaken to provide quality photographs heretofore not merely unpublished, but untaken!

Although many of the dolls and doll houses and shops thus pictured are rare and valuable, they are, to a large degree, items within reach of the average collector today. This book is fashioned with the hope of being useful to such novice collectors, as well as with the hope of furnishing stimulation to those who are more advanced.

It is true that both of the collections so thoroughly pictured here are unusual. Mrs. Faurholt has had the advantage of her location in Copenhagen, a doll-collecting territory almost pristine when she began and where other collectors are still in short supply. Her dolls epitomize what a collector today may assemble, given taste, study, luck, and much of Europe nearby. Since one continually hears that antiques of all kinds have now crossed the ocean and nothing is left abroad, the last charming convenience may not obtain for her much longer. Publication of Mrs. Faurholt's lovely pictures affords a careful look at a collection new to collectors outside of Copenhagen and one inaccessible to all save Scandinavian travelers.

As author of A History of Dolls' Houses, the writer has had the ensuing advantages of her book in building up a sizeable collection of houses, kitchens, and shops, a collection

---

[1] Flora Gill Jacobs, Scribner's, New York, 1953 and 1965, and Cassell, London, 1954.
[2] Vivien Greene, Batsford, London, 1955.

which is perhaps unusual in its variety. Almost every author has the frustrating experience of learning much more about his subject after his work is published. This one had only three doll houses at the time of publication and now has many times that number, along with considerably more information. The advantage of publication both here and abroad has lent a privileged position in which to learn of many doll houses to visit (or to collect). Some of the theories evolved by the collector in her augmented wisdom are set forth in the introduction to the doll house section. Here it seems appropriate to add that both authors share a preoccupation with the past: in finding treasures in their original condition or in restoring them thereto. We have little interest in newly be-flounced crinolines or ingeniously improvised tea cups, no matter how charming, although it is hoped that our book will be of help to both schools of doll and doll house collecting.

Just as this book will be the first published about dolls and doll houses together, it will also, we think, be one of the few in which dolls are presented in a pictorial chronology.[3] Most doll books, of course, are arranged according to doll types—waxes, woodens, papier-mâchés, and chinas—with chronology, that most precarious of all historical areas, un-attempted and with dating of any kind glossed over, if not neglected entirely. Mrs. Faurholt has had the courage, with the aid of that helpful preposition "circa," to pinpoint decades and even, when it was possible, specific years. The records of doll makers have been casual enough to make such a proceeding difficult; undoubtedly some of Mrs. Faurholt's identifications will be controversial, but all of her theories should be interesting and useful.

A doll house author cannot be as specific. Doll house furnishings often were manufactured identically, or very similarly, over a period considerably longer than a decade; and as a rule one cannot assign decades in fashions in furniture and architecture as precisely as one can in costume. Obviously people do not cast off their houses and furniture or change their styles of home decoration as often as they change their coiffures and clothes. Therefore, although it has been possible to identify early Victorian, mid-Victorian, and late Victorian in doll houses and furnishings from a study of both toy and full-sized versions and to offer a more specific date if a catalogue illustration was happily discovered, it has not been practical to provide statistics of the sort to be found in the doll section. Because of the persistence of identical patterns over a number of years, even a catalogue illustration may be no more than a guide. Dramatic instances of this truth are shown by the illustrations from a 1913 F.A.O. Schwarz catalogue which are scattered throughout the doll house section. One must be more general, but one who has been collecting and studying doll houses since 1945 may perhaps be permitted her own theories!

This book, in short, offers a chronology of fashion changes in doll bodies, heads, costumes, customs, houses, furnishings, and shops, and it provides this catalogue largely in pictures. Since, to a collector, a picture of what he collects is worth considerably more than a thousand words and is the next best thing to owning the item itself, we have chosen to present an album, with text. It is probably no coincidence that two of the most useful and most coveted books about old toys are picture books with a relatively small amount of text: Gröber's Children's Toys of Bygone Days (Batsford, 1928) and Holme's Children's Toys of Yesterday (London Studio, 1932). We use the picture-caption technique to save the wear and tear of flipping back and forth occasioned by so many such volumes.

Although this album is written by collectors for collectors, it will, we hope, be attractive and interesting to that capricious bookworm, "the general reader," as well.

F. G. J.

---

[3] Gwen White in *A Book of Dolls* has offered a more general chronology.

Contents

PART ONE

THE DOLLS

by Estrid Faurholt

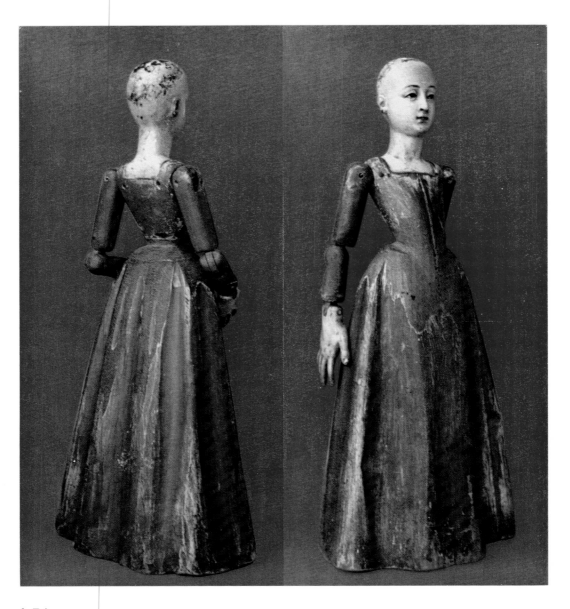

A Discovery

This doll came to the writer after most of the doll section of this book had gone to press, but since it is so extraordinary, we take the liberty of reproducing it here.

Although a date of ca. 1580 is a strong possibility, some museum experts believe this unusual doll might be Gothic.

Whether Gothic or Elizabethan, this lady is fashioned from a wooden block. Her arms move at shoulders, elbows, and wrists, and her hands are beautifully carved. Behind her painted eyes, her head is "full of thoughts."

She is 18″ tall.

Introduction

AS recently as August 1963, a New York City doll collector was thus quoted in the *New York World Telegram and Sun:* "Nobody has seen any (china dolls) with a Danish mark and the Royal Copenhagen porcelain factory has no record of any being made there." The collection pictured herewith shows three heads with the Royal Copenhagen mark, all of them attested to by the Copenhagen factory! Another picture provided through the courtesy of the factory itself shows models of nine others.

This example may serve as well as any to demonstrate the amount of confusion that exists about dolls, even among knowledgeable collectors. Many collectors are studying dolls; much information has been printed in the past; a great deal may be impossible to learn. But as each book and article appears, more will be discovered. It is the belief of the authors of this book that since the best way to learn about an elusive subject is to study the objects themselves, we can do no better than to offer these objects in pictures—as many as possible and as clear as photography can make them.

Although the oldest doll shown in this collection is from the sixteenth century and there are more than a few from the eighteenth, the dolls pictured, for the most part, are from the nineteenth, a century in which dolls of good quality became available for the first time to little girls in families of moderate means. Such children prized their dolls and took good care of them; many have survived, unless they were carelessly handed down to the more casual young doll mothers of recent years. It is these nineteenth-century dolls which are the most popular among collectors, as well as the most readily available.

Rather than divide them according to types—waxes, parians, chinas, and such, in the style of the majority of doll books to date, we offer them chronologically, hoping at the same time to present a procession of hair styles, dress styles, and other fashions along with a hint of their sociological implications. But for all the implications, sociological and otherwise, which may appear, the writers are primarily concerned with presenting an album—one which will help collectors to date their own dolls but which will also be a picture book of the past.

Most of these dolls have come, dressed in their original clothes and accompanied by their histories, from their original families. A large percentage were found in the writer's native Denmark where doll collectors are rare and where assembling such a collection, therefore, has been less competitive than in other countries where the hobby has been more popular and assiduous.

Although some general doll information has been given in the captions themselves, a brief glossary of doll terms will be found at the end of this section. There are, of course, many books containing general doll information; this one, however, hopes to pictorialize and particularize rather than generalize. Therefore we shall dwell as little as possible on the sort of doll information which has been published elsewhere and often. Nevertheless, a generalization or two from this collector's own experience of studying dolls in museums in various European countries may be helpful.

Above each caption, the writer has designated, to the best of her knowledge, the period of the doll which it describes. It would have been gratifying to have been able to indicate the country of origin as well, but one cannot often say of a doll, as one can of a plate, that it is German or French or English. Perhaps the body was made in Germany and the head in Denmark; it may have been dressed by an aunt in Sweden and sent to a little girl in England. Which country then can claim the doll's origin? It has been possible only to say that most china heads with black-painted headdresses are German, whereas wooden dolls or dolls with wax, papier-mâché, bisque, or parian heads were made in various countries, as the captions describing the ones pictured suggest. Many doll collectors have wondered if black-haired chinas were once made at Staffordshire as these doll heads greatly resemble Staffordshire porcelains in style, but so far no proof has been found.

The dress of the doll is often a help in dating the doll. Not many little girls want a doll with an old-fashioned dress. Most children dislike antiques—they want to have the same things their friends have, and generation after generation has put its toys aside to let a new little girl have a new little doll. Occasionally, though, a doll was handed down and given a new dress with the new generation, and one must be wary. There is sometimes a puzzler in reverse, such as the French lady in Color Plate 5, one of whose shoes has, in tiny writing on its sole, "Tante Elise, Sept. 1852," but who is herself, along with the rest of her clothing, ca. 1875. It is obvious then that one cannot always be *positive,* but many a grandchild may have come across Grandma's doll or even Great-grandma's doll in the attic on a rainy day and thought it ridiculous, and let it remain there. Such rejections were a help to collectors and to history!

As the writer has indicated, she began doll collecting in Denmark (and Europe) when this branch of collecting was still new—and one could still find those who had an old and unwanted doll in a drawer. A bit of information nearly always accompanied the doll and added to the store of material for this book.

It is such tales which give doll collecting much of its charm. Many touching stories come from the dolls' original "families." One day there was even a rather macabre visit from a churchyard employee who had found a lovely 1840 doll's head and legs and arms, all china, in a grave he was digging. The recipient was somewhat troubled by the origin of this present, but it is now among her treasures where it is a wistful but touching reminder of an unknown child who was buried with her doll in her arms.

When the two-faced doll (Plate 103) was acquired, a price was asked which seemed rather high, but the writer paid without comment and was rewarded by the owner's heartfelt thanks and this foot-note: "I had decided that my daughter should be permitted to go to college if I got that sum for the doll—it would be a sort of sign for me." Ever since, the two-faced doll has been a happy reminder that perhaps a life has been more rewarding because of her.

It has been a pleasure to remain in contact with many of the people who parted with their dolls. Every Christmas at least a letter tells the former owner how the departed one is faring. This is also reversed. From an old fisherman on a Danish island, an annual greeting comes to Jacqueline, a lovely parian with glass eyes, of whom he said when he sold her years ago, "I shall be longing for her, but nobody can forbid me to think about her." The writer sent him a picture of Jacqueline which, during a brief visit, she later saw on the wall above his bed.

The first dolls surely were sticks and stones or even rags, primitive pathetic little creatures, but loved by the little girls who nursed them. Later came dolls of clay and wood which were made as late as the nineteenth century. Wax heads were made during the eighteenth and nineteenth centuries, and in some of the later ones, the wax was a thin coating over papier-mâché, a material which came into use for doll heads around 1815. China heads are believed to have originated ca. 1825, and china was from then on the preferred material for heads, either glazed or unglazed. The latter occurred in the form of parian or bisque, a substance in which both Germany and France fashioned lovely heads.

Although most of the china heads were made in Germany, it is a pleasure, to revert to the opening paragraph of this brief introduction, to reveal some hitherto unreported information about lovely china heads made in Denmark. The books of the Royal Danish Porcelain Factory in Copenhagen list twelve different heads made from 1844–84. The quality of the heads, all of which have brown painted-on headdresses and were made in various sizes, is very fine. Three Royal Copenhagens in the writer's collection may be seen in this book. Through the courtesy of Mr. Grandjean of the Royal Copenhagen Porcelain Factory, nine heads in the possession of the company are also shown and their marks pictured.

Speaking more personally, I wish to take this opportunity to thank two people who helped to make the doll section of this book possible: Dagny Screeton, until recently the only other doll collector here in Denmark, with whom I shared many instructive hours in which we studied and examined dolls; and Flora Gill Jacobs, my collaborator, who re-wrote and edited my material. I began as a collector of doll houses rather than dolls and thought I was the only doll house collector in the world till, with joy, I saw Mrs. Jacobs' book, *A History of Dolls' Houses,* in 1954. When I wrote to thank Mrs. Jacobs for her book, a correspondence ensued which resulted in this book. I wish also to thank Vivien Greene, author of *English Dolls' Houses,* with whom I have shared many friendly and instructive hours exploring our mutual interests of dolls and doll houses.

Thanks also, to Mr. Claus Næraa for his never-ending care and skill in taking the pictures for my section of the book.

When this book appears, I shall not, needless to say, stop studying dolls, and perhaps its publication will be of help in pursuing my research. Information from readers will be welcomed. Serious doll research has been neglected for so long, especially in Europe, that it is necessary to try to work hard now—before it is too late and possible nuggets of information are covered over forever.

Estrid Faurholt
Strandvejen 229 B
Charlottenlund

List of Plates: Part One

COLOR PLATES

BLACK & WHITE

Before 1820

1 Venerable Doll; late seventeenth century; 15½" high

The oldest doll in this book,* this wooden personage with horsehair wig and glass eyes is believed to date from between 1650 and 1700. Her arms and legs are missing, but her head and torso are of particular interest. Her eyes are brown with black pupils, and she has the flat back typical of these dolls. Gwen White, in *A Book of Dolls* (A. and C. Black Ltd., 1956), pictures several of these flat-back dolls and shows a cross-section of the glass rod from which their eyes were made. A very thin layer of paint, interestingly faded by the centuries, gives our doll a subtle coloring.

She comes from England and is rare even apart from her age. The Great Plague cost the lives of nearly as many dolls as children; the pitiful treasures of deceased little owners, of course, had to be thrown into the plague pits.

It is unusual to find a doll in which the sex is indicated.

* Since these words were printed, the doll in the frontispiece has, of course, been added.

2 Early Wooden from France; *ca.* 1730–1740; 10½" high

This imposing personage with her baroque features is undoubtedly unique and is believed to date as early as the third decade of the eighteenth century.

Found in Paris, she is fashioned entirely of wood with limbs articulated at the shoulders, wrists, hips, and knees. Her painted-on stockings are red (stockings after ca. 1740 tend to be white), and her yellowish shoes have red heels. The silver brocade skirt of her dress, which is stiffened with red baize, is trimmed with gold lace; its tight bodice of matching fabric is embroidered with gold and silver threads.

One wonders if this most interesting doll was one of those long-ago fashion dolls sent from Paris to the courts of Europe to show "La Mode." Such dolls were known as early as 1396 when King Charles VI of France sent dolls with costly wardrobes to his daughter, the Queen of England, second wife of Richard II. Even in the first decade of the eighteenth century, when the two countries were at war, fashion dolls were sent from France to England.

Color Plate 1: Doll from 1690; 13½″ high

This remarkable jointed wooden, her blue eyes and high cheeks delicately painted, is of the Queen Anne period, and her dress of satin and gold lace embroidery would appear to pre-date the doll. Her lace cap and undergarments are original, though it would seem that the petticoat of buckram was added in Victorian times to suit the fashion, and modesty, of that period.

Her delicately carved wooden fingers clad in kidskin gloves and her wooden feet are characteristic of dolls of the period, as is her wasp waist. Her wig, natural golden hair of delicate texture, is sewn to a rather rough piece of linen shaped to the skull, stitched, and nailed—typical of doll-making of the time. She has no less than eight beauty spots painted on her face.

Color Plate 2: Two Japanese Dolls; *ca.* 1750; 5½″ high

These two charming *gosho-ningyo* dolls, from the middle of the Edo period (1603–1868), have been chosen to represent a number of dolls the author added to her collection on a resent visit to Japan. As *gosho*, which means "palace," suggests, the dolls are from Kyoto, where the royal residence was at the time they were made. Their smooth glistening surface results from the application of layers of *gofun* (powdered sea shells) and a glue called *nikawa* to wood. The resulting finish is dried and polished till this lovely sheen is achieved. Such dolls were used as presents even by the Emperor who is said to have bought a certain number every year to give to newborn babies and to ladies as talismen when traveling. The earliest dolls were made for ceremonial purposes (see Plate 217, doll house section), and play dolls of course came later.

The toy held by the larger doll has been explained by two discrepant interpretations. One is that this is a "treasure cart," into which all the wishes for the child's future life are placed; the other asserts that the doll commemorates an illustrious boy who was so strong that he could draw a heavy cart up to the very peak of a high mountain.

3 Eighteenth-Century Wax Head;
ca. 1773; 5″ high

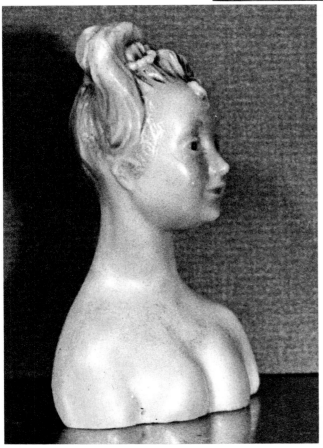

Unquestionably this wax head is unique, with only an artist likely to have created a piece of such delicacy and beauty. The lady's expression is lovely, as is the way in which she holds her head, which is molded in wax of natural color with no pink added. Some pearls and a bow are molded into her elegant coiffure.

That she is from the eighteenth century seemed obvious, but a more precise date was a question. The doll detective began to work on the matter, and one day she saw an old painting of a lady with exactly the same headdress. That lady was painted in 1773. . . .

4 Dancing Doll; *ca.* 1760; 2¼″ high

This small conversation piece is a dancing doll. All of wood and beautifully painted, his little face is nicely carved. He is hollow, enabling his legs, hung by string within his body, to move freely. He stands on four bristles just stiff enough to hold him upright. When placed on a piano, he really can dance—if someone plays! Perhaps there were eight of these small figures, four men and four women, dancing a quadrille and creating much merriment.

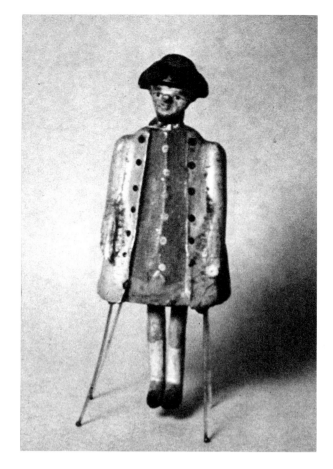

5 Baby in a Golden Bed; seventeenth century; length of bed, 8½″

This baby is accompanied by a printed label which looks as though it might have come from a museum. In Italian, this identifies it as "Doll with terra cotta head, lying in handmade gilded bed. Seventeenth century."

Lying on a green silk mattress and a pillow trimmed with handmade silver lace, the baby wears swaddling clothes which have evidently been renewed, as they are trimmed with Valenciennes of a later date. If these are removed, there is only a terra cotta torso—no arms or legs. The baby has dark, glass eyes without pupils in the fashion of dolls' glass eyes of the period.

A carved angel with wings outstretched forms the footboard of the bed, and one wonders if this was from a very elaborate Christmas crèche or was perhaps for the Christ child in some church, given as an offering in exchange for help from Mary.

6 Wax Doll on a Stick; *ca.* 1790; 6½″ high

The whole body of this slender creature, found in Paris, consists of a wooden stick. She has over-sized wax hands and black pearl eyes in her wax head with its molded hair. Since her striped cotton dress is glued to parchment, it is stiff enough to keep her upright.

The old Danish bride's chest, dated "1791," is painted green. A verse on the lid tells of Maren who shall wear the clothes inside with "virginal pride" (an approximate translation).

Dated "1716," the silver candelabrum is from Amsterdam, and the pitcher, also Dutch, is dated "1756." The kettle is not marked, but is another early bit of silver.

7 Wooden Actress; *ca.* 1780; 29″ high

She hung on the wall by a string round her neck, but nevertheless she smiled. Purchase was essential—and prompt. This took place in the Marché Biron in Paris.

She is a very interesting creature with dark brown eyes and a completely lifelike face. When photographed, she offered as many different expressions as there were pictures. Carved entirely in wood except for her arms which are of stuffed linen wired for bendability, she has beautifully carved hands and feet. Microscopic examination reveals that a small hole has been filled in each hand and foot suggesting that she has been an "actress"—a marionette.

Judging by her dress, she is from Brittany, or that was her role as an actress. She has a dark complexion, a red and white striped cotton petticoat, a flowered quilted cretonne skirt, and a blouse, apron, and shawl of nice old printed cotton.

8 Patricia; *ca.* 1760; 14″ high

This rare lady, obviously from the mid-eight-eenth century, has extraordinary jewels painted on her composition head with its painted-on powdered wig. Her elaborate earrings and the dog collar, with its splendid clasp which matches a clasp in her pompadour, are painted yellow instead of the usual gold, with red and green for the stones. A hole above her left ear causes one to suspect that she may have worn a real jewel there. She has the finest wasp waist the author has ever seen, legs with painted-on green shoes which have bands criss-crossing to bows at the top, and painted-on red garters. Her body is of linen.

Although her dress is nice and suits the fashion of ca. 1760, it probably was made no more than a hundred years ago. The doll herself is very, very interesting and lovely, and the author, who has never seen anything like her, would be delighted to hear from anyone who has.

9 Frances; *ca.* 1800; 15¼″ high

This composition-headed lady with painted eyes and linen body comes from France and, her headdress reveals, from a part of Brittany called Morbihan. Her white stockings and velvet boots are sewn to her body, and she wears a brown silk dress with black lace shawl and black lace mittens. (No fingers are indicated on her hands.) On the crown of her head, a big black dot is painted, and under her headdress she wears a cap of brown velvet. She is very well preserved.

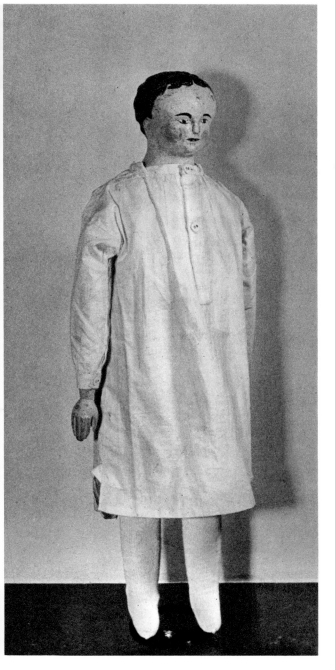

10 Dutch Wooden Man; *ca.* 1790–1800; 22½″ high

This gentleman, bought in Holland, is a typical example of the treasures to be found in wooden dolls made there from the seventeenth to the eighteenth centuries (and surely before as well). He's a bit more primitive than most of the English, French, Spanish, and Italian dolls of that time; Dutch dolls of that period are more like the Scandinavian and German, but each has its own unmistakable character.

This man with short hair is from around 1800, perhaps a little earlier. He has arms and hands of wood, and legs of the same linen as his body. It is thought that Dutch wooden dolls did not have wooden legs until after 1860.

When the writer acquired this doll, it was dressed as a woman, complete with corset and corset-hider, a curious item in use in Holland around 1870. But under its garment was the man's shirt pictured, handmade and beautifully cut. The writer looked at the doll and its big wooden hands and decided to let him remain in his shirt, and, to liberate him from his anachronistic feminine garb.

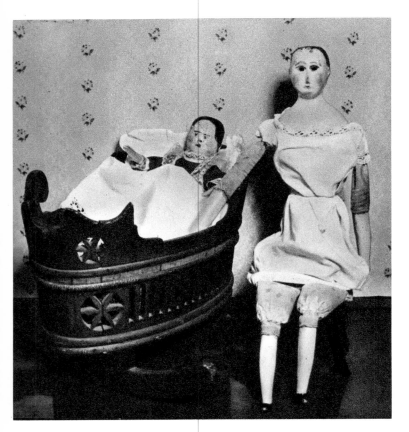

11 Measles & Dried Peas; *ca.* 1800; 21½″

The hand that rocks the cradle here is hand-carved, and so are the legs and the head of this early Danish doll with body of hand-woven linen. She has been photographed without her dress to reveal a distressing, but amusing, condition. She has measles—at least this seems the most reasonable diagnosis of the little red spots all over her body. Presumably her young owner had measles and it seemed appropriate for her doll to have them too. She also has a suitable complexion for a shut-in, the same faded gray paint found on old wooden church-figures of the same period.

A Dutch collector and expert recently advanced the theory that when the hair on a wooden doll is "combed" away from the face, the doll is eighteenth century. If true, this doll is earlier than 1800.

The child in the cradle is of the more usual jointed-wooden type, and her cradle is as amusing as her mother's unfortunate spots. It has a double bottom, with dried peas between the two layers—a built-in rattle when the cradle is rocked. A similar cradle in full-size may be seen in the Danish National Museum.

12 Doll with Sedan Chair I; *ca.* 1800; sedan chair, *ca.* 1740; height of chair; 4½″

Under her pink silk-banded turban, of the same fine and fragile fabric as her dress, she has a nicely-painted head with black hair. She can move her jointed limbs freely at the hips, knees, shoulders, and elbows. A bit of old lace trims her dress, which in addition to her turban is all she wears. According to the fashion of the time, the Empire period from 1804–15, underwear was at a minimum, pantalettes being unknown. Our wooden lady might also have worn a chemise and possibly a petticoat, but that was all.

The sedan chair, covered in a hand-woven brownish print with painted touches of yellow, may be as early as 1740. The interior is lined in silk and velvet of a subtle pinkish brown.

13 Old Danish Wooden; date uncertain;
9½″ high

Found among junk in a Northseeland shop,
this primitive doll certainly was made before
1800, perhaps considerably before. It is difficult
to date such a doll. It is turned of beechwood,
with features carved afterwards, and several old
hand-wrought nails remain to indicate how the
wig was fastened. Under them, traces of the
material used for the wig itself may be per-
ceived. This fabric may have been lamb's wool,
but one cannot be positive.

The 1820's

14 Fortune Teller; *ca.* 1820; 10" high

This seems a typical Biedermeier doll, ca. 1830, till her coat is opened. Then she becomes the ultimate conversation piece. Anyone wishing to read the future need only read one of the paper panels (tied with a string about her small waist) which form her underskirt. If one panel says that the fortune-seeker will never marry, one need only select another. Perhaps that panel will reveal that one will marry happily twice. Since there are sixty-four panels, there is a good possibility of finding an attractive future.

The panels are inscribed in Danish Gothic letters, a clue to this Nordic gypsy's past. Beneath her prescient skirt, she has a body delicately fashioned of fine kidskin. Her head is of papier-mâché, her arms and legs are of wood, and her hair is painted on with a bit of black felt sewn to her gypsy turban for bangs.

15 Baby from 1820; 1″ high

This tiny creature came to her present owner with a letter indicating that she dates from 1820. Her long dress, much longer than the baby herself, is obviously original. Her sash (talk of tiny waists!) is red and has an elaborate bow in back. Underneath the dress, she has a petticoat wonderfully embroidered and similarly embellished with fine lace. The petticoat has been painstakingly monogrammed M.F., with the name these initials represent forever lost.

This baby really does have a body underneath! She is entirely of wood, but her arms and legs lack the joints of many similar wooden dolls.

16 Beatrice; *ca.* 1825; 31″ high

One of the earliest of the sleeping-eye dolls, this lady happily has a hole in her wax head for fastening her wig—happily, because this hole enabled her owner to peer inside after having gotten a notion about her eyes. A little rust hole in her back was a clue that a lever, now missing, had once emerged there. Inside the head, a wire mechanism which enabled the lever to open and shut the doll's eyes may be seen.

Beatrice is as much as 140 years old, and she certainly has some age lines, but at her age one seems entitled to a few. Her wig, which she came by at some point in her life, is made with long curls falling about her shoulders (here pinned up for a better view of the head). Her body is of linen, and she wears an old silk dress ornamented with real lace.

17 Terra Cotta Head; 1850 or earlier; 4″ high

A terra cotta head is quite rare, and it is likely that this one is from South Germany or Italy and is probably the head of a crèche doll from the middle of the nineteenth century. She has brown glass eyes and an unusually lifelike expression—kindly and understanding. The strange thickness of her neck suggests to the doll detective that she may have come from one of those South German valleys where many of the inhabitants have a glandular illness caused by a lack of iodine in the diet.

18 The Duchess of Kent; *ca.* 1825; 20½″

A label was pinned to the dress of the Duchess when she was found: "Said to be portrait doll of Queen Victoria's mother, the Duchess of Kent." Early portrait dolls are believed to be exceedingly rare, but even if this is not a portrait, it is a lovely papier-mâché. With her interesting, exaggerated coiffure, she is ca. 1825.

The Duchess also wears her original dress from ca. 1825–30, a wonderful cream-colored silk with sleeves full at the shoulders and a wasp waist. Around the hem of the skirt, a band of the silk is caught in scallops by delicate rosettes, and a tasseled sash is at her waist. She wears red gloves and shoes of the same material as her dress, and she carries a reticule.

Color Plate 3: Empire Doll; *ca.* 1820; 16″ high

This unusual milliner's model has one of the earliest of papier-mâché heads, *ca.* 1820 perhaps. She is Empire, or just after, with her dark-brown hair braided into a coronet above her lovely pink-cheeked face. A pair of curls fall casually on her forehead and her ears are free.

She has a fine kid body and her kidskin fingers are separated. On her feet she wears shoes of the same light blue silk as her dress. Russian in aspect, the latter appears to be a sort of peasant dress sewn for a nobleman's daughter, and therefore not of wool but of the finest silk available.

On the table, a tea urn, a pair of Delft decanters, and a lovely Venetian glass are at the disposal of this appealing doll.

The 1830's

19 Drawing Room; *ca.* **1830; about 12″ high**

We find in this drawing room not only what the well-dressed doll was wearing in 1830 but also what she was made of, inasmuch as one of these ladies' heads is of porcelain, one is of papier-mâché, and one (with her back turned) is of wood. Despite these differences, the dolls have more in common than their age: long, slender, kid bodies with wooden arms and legs, the latter terminating in painted-on red shoes. A clue which enables the knowing collector to distinguish such Empire dolls from later ones is the colored strip of fabric which conceals the fastening of the limbs. Since the small doll on the sofa, entirely of wood and jointed, is from about 1800, she may be seated in deference to her status as a member of an older generation!

The attractive handmade garments worn by these ladies include chemises with little sleeves, pantalettes, and at least two petticoats beneath their embroidered dresses; and all wear bonnets of lace and tulle. However, the wooden-headed lady of fashion may out-do her contemporaries with the elegance of a coat over her dress and her net bag containing her handkerchief.

The somewhat anachronistic chandelier is about 1850, but the candlestand behind the dolls is a true antique even to these dolls' generation. Of silver, it is marked with a precision of which doll collectors, as a rule, can only dream—marks asserting year and place of origin: "Amsterdam, 1716."

20 Bedroom; *ca.* 1820–30; (tallest doll) 10″ high

About to retire to her Danish four poster (and probably on a frigid Danish winter evening), milady, ca. 1830, models the several garments one did well to wear for slumber in the days before central heating. First she dons a knitted vest, and then her chemise, which is long and has tiny sleeves. Over that she wears her heavy linen bedjacket which criss-crosses in front for extra warmth and is belted. Her lace-frilled nightcap is embroidered.

The wooden doll at the foot of the bed, ca. 1820 (as is her striped dress), has two wooden dolls of her own.

Both bed and shaving mirror are of mahogany, but the chest is a surprise; it is metal, painted to resemble wood. A Victorian scrap screen from England is an interesting accessory.

21 Dresses from the 1820's–30's

Three of the dresses shown are ca. 1830, and the one at the right, with its very high waistline and puffed sleeves, is ca. 1820. The item in the foreground is a bedjacket.

In 1830, sleeves were very full at the shoulders, waists at their normal level, and skirts wide. If shoulders were bare, one modestly wore a little cape to hide them when away from home.

Undergarments at the time were of fine lawn with neither lace nor frills; only quality was essential. Pantalettes had just come into use in 1830 and were open, being joined only at the waistband.

22 *Early Danish Kitchen; ca.* 1820; 18½″ high

The papier-mâché lady of the house and her young porcelain-headed maid, both ca. 1830, preside over a rare old Danish kitchen from the south of Jutland. With its nice old bluegreen walls and brown and beige checkerboard floor, the kitchen, ca. 1820, has its original furnishings. An unusual feature is a sort of butler's pantry which is a small adjoining room (see detail).

It is intriguing not only to note that the furniture is of teak, but also to speculate that it was probably brought from Jutland's western coast by some sea captain who sailed to the Far East and brought home tea and spices in boxes which later were fashioned into these small treasures for his children.

The container with funnel (foreground) is for kerosene used to light the lamps in the house. Since kerosene did not come into commercial production till the 'fifties, it is likely that this item found its way into the kitchen later. The English pottery soup tureen on the table is decorated. Nearly everything else is of brass, copper, or tin. Unfortunately, the copper water tank which was built into the outer wall of the kitchen and connected to a spout inside has disappeared.

The mistress of this fine display has a linen body stuffed with lamb's wool and a head of papier-mâché. Her arms are very primitive, being thin rolls of linen. She wears stockings with green silk garters, and her dress is a nice faded red. Her servant has body, arms, hands, and legs of kid and wears a smart checked dress with cape collar.

23 Mrs. Pease; *ca.* 1830; 16½″ high

When this early English papier-mâché with lovely clothes and fine bonnet came to the owner, she was a blonde and looked quite puzzling. The former owner had mounted a blonde wig on a piece of linen and glued this to the head, undoubtedly because the head had been broken and this was holding it in place. When this wig was removed, there was revealed a lovely, early Victorian, black coiffure molded on, with center part, bun in back, and ears showing.

Her head is fixed, and her body very light, possibly stuffed with lamb's wool as were so many at that time.

24 Tilting Doll; *ca.* 1830; 5¼″ high

A traditional toy that spans the ages, this amusing old tilting doll, being carefully weighted to remain upright, won't lie down, try her as you will. She is made of papier-mâché, and her roly-poly shape replaces the legs of a more conventional doll, a fact which is hidden under her blue skirt. Doll, dress, bonnet, and baby whom she holds so lovingly are molded together. The colors are faded, but one can see clearly how nice they originally were—white bonnet with blue band, red shawl, and blue dress.

Tilting dolls can be traced to the Orient of long ago and are believed to have a religious origin. It is said of Brahma that he never could fall, and the symbolism is readily discernible. In China the tilting doll was often found in the guise of an old man with a fan who was identified with the phrase, "Stand up little Priest." In Japan such dolls are called *daruma* after an ancient Buddhist sage who came over from India in the sixth century and, it is said, spent the next nine years sitting in "umbilicular meditation." The bright-eyed version of our photograph, far removed from these beginnings, has a Cockney look about her.

25 Wooden Biedermeier Doll; *ca.* 1830; 17½″ high

She is no beauty, but she is charming and funny with her wooden head, bun at the neck carved in one piece with the head, and her wooden arms and legs. A light layer of gesso under the paint has given her face a realistic texture.

Her body is a very old linen one with a squeak-box inside. She wears a chemise and an old flowered shawl and, as her skirt is missing, only her two petticoats are under her little apron. Especially amusing are her blue boots painted with little white dots for buttons.

26 Doll with Sedan Chair II; *ca.* 1830; 10″ high

The chic personage who has just stepped from her very elegant sedan chair has a kid body with head, arms, and legs of wood. Her similarly wooden coiffure features a bun at the neck. Since she comes from Paris, presumably her dress and hat, which like her undergarments are as old as she, were high fashion when they were made. Her blouse is of mauve taffeta, and her fringed pink apron is also of silk. Her bonnet is quite marvelous, being fashioned of the most delicate silk, its poke seamed and shaped with infinitesimal wires.

Charmingly painted with delicate flowers, birds, and scrolls, the wooden sedan chair is gorgeously lined in white brocade. It is earlier than the doll.

27 Ane, an Early China; *ca.* 1830; 22″ high

Ane is a china-headed doll from around 1830. There are some heads from about 1860 which look very much like hers, but if one studies her hairdo one notes that her vertical curls fall freely about her head and neck and do not cling to the head like the ones of the 'sixties.

   She looks as if she came from the country, and her clothes suit a farmer's wife. Her red cotton dress has an underskirt of the same material, similarly black-banded at the seam. The dress is later than the doll, perhaps from 1850–60, but of course a doll was likely to be given a new dress when she came to a new owner. She carries a knitted shawl, and her white stockings are nicely knitted too.

The 1840's

28 Cavalcade of Coiffures; 1840–80

Five decades of coiffures, from (left) 1840 to (right) 1880, are represented in this informative group. As the picture suggests, 1840's ladies (this one is papier-mâché) showed high foreheads; in 1850 they permitted a wave or two to intrude; in 1860, let the hair dip lower on the forehead; in 1870, became quite gay and allowed ringlets and other miscellaneous curls to lower it some more; and in 1880, sanctioned bangs down to the very eyes.

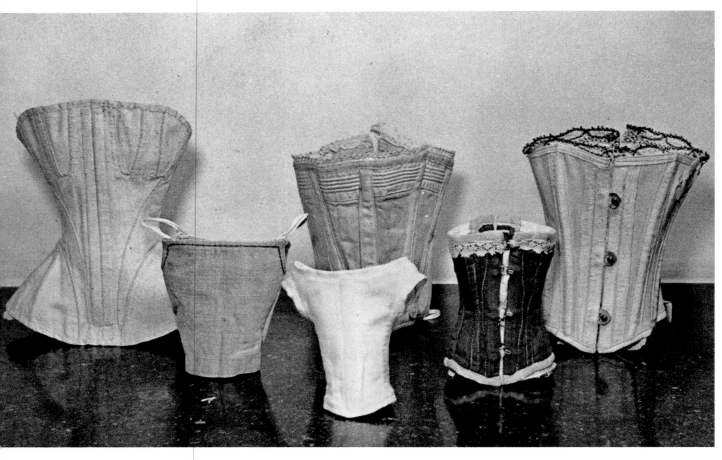

29 Various Corsets; nineteenth century, highest 6½″

If one studies these interesting corsets, all of them from the nineteenth century, one can readily judge that at least two of them belong to dresses with wasp waists and wide skirts. The earliest, ca. 1800, has shoulder straps and reaches only to the waist. The white one (center) with short sleeves is from ca. 1830 and is wonderfully shaped with tiny ribs which may be removed when it is washed. The corset (left rear) from ca. 1844 is of coarse fabric, but the workmanship is marvelous. Of course it is hand-sewn (the sewing machine not having been invented), and the shape is perfect, with metal eyelets in the back for lacing. (Such eyelets were first used ca. 1828.) The corset ca. 1860 (second from right) is, as was the fashion, red. Next to it (right rear) is one from ca. 1894, an excellent foundation for a Gay 'Nineties dress.

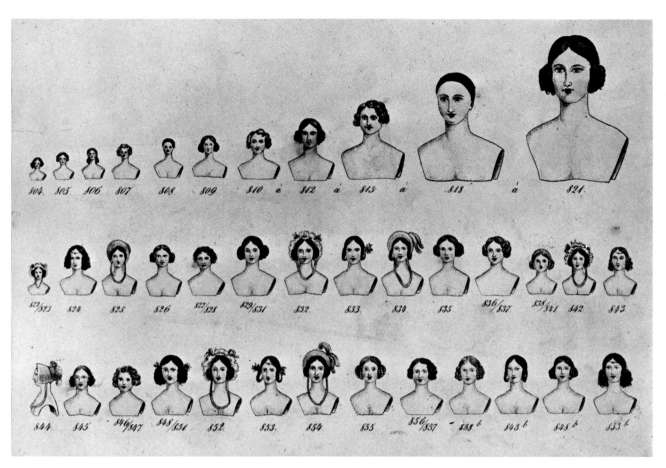

30 Miscellany of Dolls in a German Toy Catalogue; *ca.* 1848

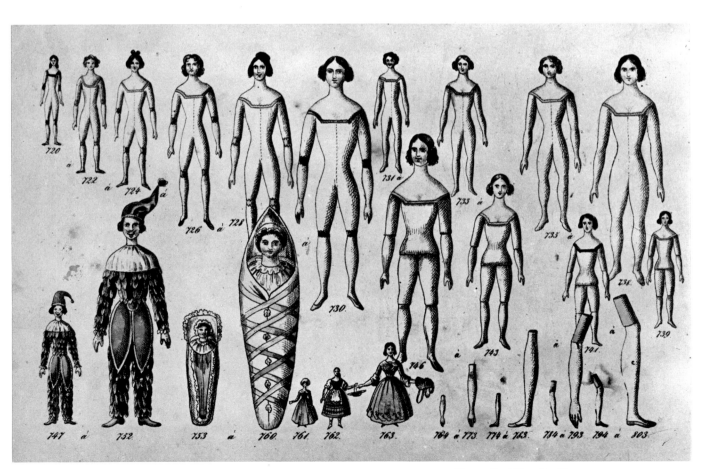

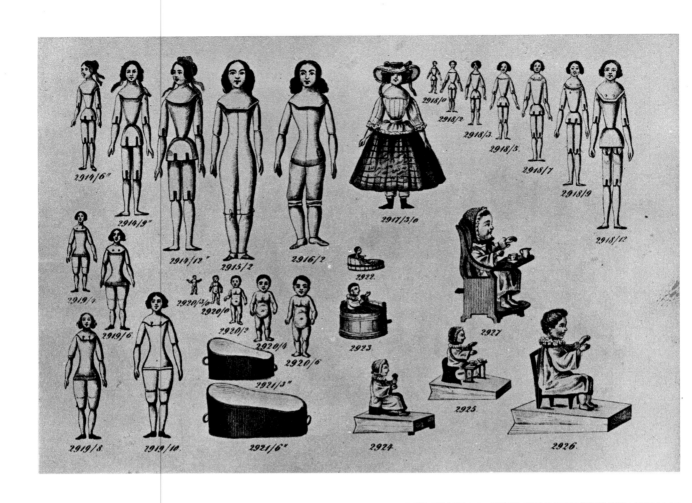

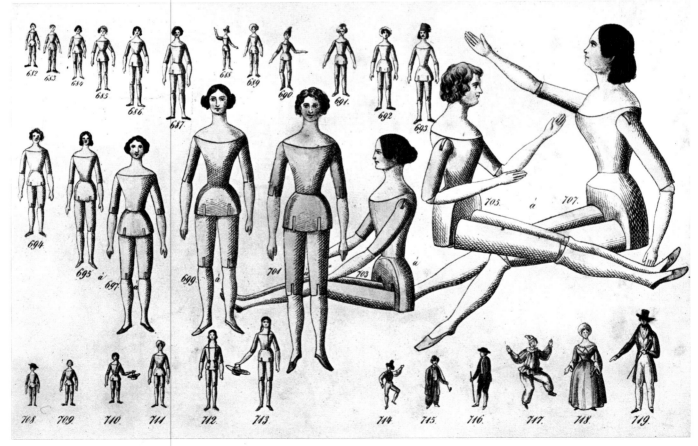

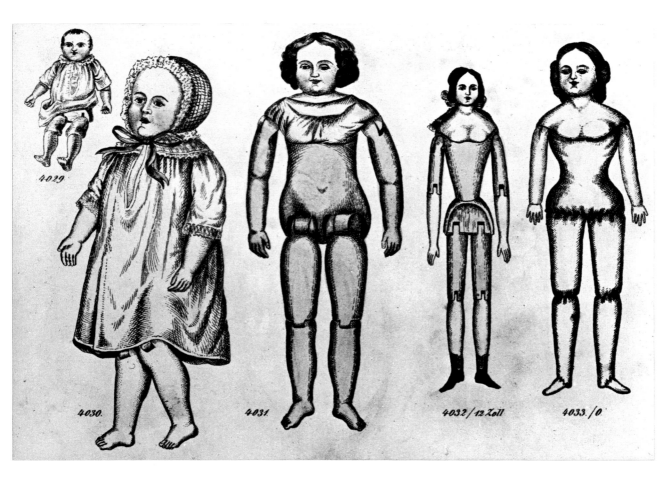

4029.

4030.

4031.

4032./12 Zoll

4033. /0

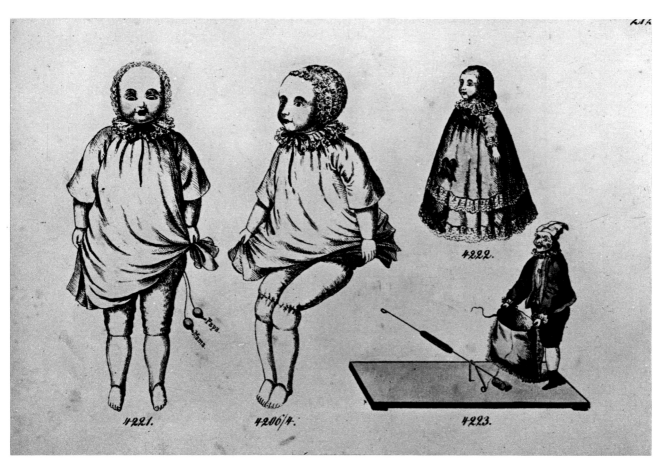

4221.

4206/4.

4222.

4223.

31 Plaster Models from the Royal Copenhagen Factory; 1844–84

The remarkable picture, shown through the courtesy of the Royal Copenhagen Factory, shows casts of nine of the twelve different heads made, in various sizes, by the factory during the period 1844–1884. It is believed that few are still in existence. The writer has seen seven during her years as a collector (and resident of Copenhagen), and the only known specimen of the head at left rear is in her own collection (Plate 32). Before it was found in an antique shop some years ago, factory officials had not seen a head like it, and no other has appeared since.

The head at right rear is the head of the doll shown in Plate 33. The head of the doll in Plate 34 did not exist in the collection of models but only as a damaged china head. No record has been found so far to indicate in detail when the various heads were made, but perhaps further research will bring that information to light. When these heads are found, they have one of three marks:

The only fact relating to date which is known is that the dot above the lines indicates a date before 1850. The dot seldom occurs even in dolls obviously made before 1850, but when it does, the early date is conclusive.

It is interesting to note that a boy's head (lower right) was among those made.

32 Julie, a Royal Copenhagen; *ca.* 1840; 4″ high

This rare head comes from the Royal Copenhagen porcelain factory and might very well have been, to judge by the early headdress, the first ever made in that factory. The mark inside the head, the factory's customary three wavelines (occasionally three straight lines) has a dot above the lines that indicates a date before 1850 (see Plate 34).

Remarkably enough, Mr. Bredo Grandjean, director of the museum and archivist of the Royal Copenhagen factory, says that he has never seen another head like this one. He thinks this lady may have been made before 1844, even though the records fail to confirm such a judgment.

This coiffure with a bun on top and side curls, fashionable as early as the late 1820's, is a rich brown, as are all Royal Copenhagen coiffures.

33 Amalie, another Copenhagen; *ca.* 1840; 22″ high

This lovely Royal Copenhagen head—marked with three straight lines—came with her history, appropriately enough from the family of a Danish Bishop.

Amalie's brown hair has the usual 1840 hairdo with center part and bun at neck. She has the customary blue eyes and the same fine coloring and texture as Julie (Plate 32). Her undergarments are also ca. 1840, and her dress is probably original too. She has wooden arms and legs.

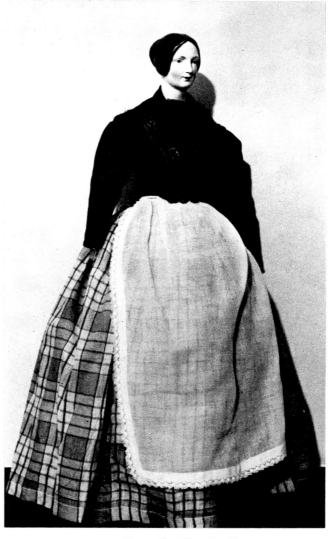

Part I: The Dolls 41

34 Signe, another Copenhagen; *ca.* 1844; 13¾″ high

Although Signe is the most finely dressed doll in the author's collection, it is not her clothes but her head which is her most arresting feature. Another of the Royal Copenhagen heads, this one is marked (inside) with three lines and a dot, the mark used before 1850. This small beauty has a center part in her coiffure which dips high over the ears and ends in a bun at the back with a little curl behind each ear. Such dolls are difficult to find, even in Denmark.

As for Signe's clothes, every thing is absolutely perfect. Her name is embroidered on her undergarments, her underskirts and chemise are made with great care, and her corset, which is pictured in Plate 29, has shoulder pieces of the type used as early as 1830. Her pink dress, of the fabric we'd today call voile, has, of course, a lined bodice and lace at neck and wrists. The latter also have the tiniest buttons and button-holes one might hope to see—if one can see them!

It is interesting to note that this head is not to be found among the remarkable collection of Copenhagen factory models shown in Plate 31.

35 Berlin Doll; 1840; 16″ high

This girl may be in peasant dress, but she is of royal porcelain! Her head inside is marked with a scepter in blue and the letters "KPM," Königliche Porzellan Manufactur, in black (all underglaze). The fact that there are no periods after the initials indicates that she was made prior to 1844. Her short brown hair, with its center part and without the bun which one might expect at the neck, is most unusual.

Her dress is unmistakably a peasant's, but as her bonnet and shawl are gone, it is not possible to know what German region she represents. Her dress is of dark wool, but her apron of old French brocade glistens in rich and luminous colors.

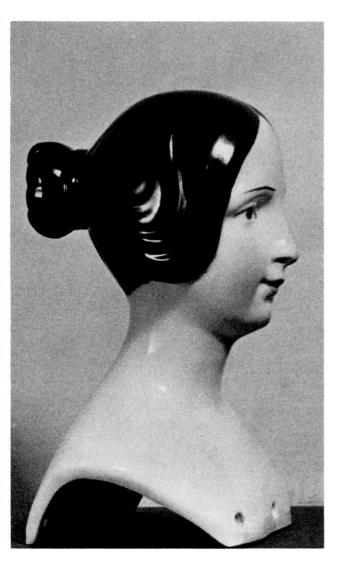

36 Berlin Head; *ca.* 1840; 6¼″ high

This pink lustre head the author believes to be
the loveliest in her collection. The brown hair has
a most unusual coiffure with its "band" around
the protruding bun, and the face has the nicest
expression.

There are two marks inside the head. One, in
blue, is a scepter with "KPM" beneath it. The
second consists of a red circle with a blue "KPM"
beneath. These marks indicate that this is a
Berlin head, ca. 1840.

37 Another KPM; 1847–49; 6″ high

This unpainted boy's head is a Berlin head. Although the owner was told that it was a girl's, *all*
girls and women in 1847–49, when this head was
made, had hair with a center part, whereas boys
and men all had side parts. And, of course, men
did wear their hair long. (This boy's ears may be
seen.)

Inside the head, in dark blue and black, may
be found a circle surrounding an eagle, with
"Königliche Porzellan Manufactur" spelled out
inside and around the rim. This is a Berlin mark
used between 1847 and 1849.

38 Meissen Doll; *ca.* 1830–40; 13″ high

This lovely doll with her golden hair, brown eyes, and fine coloring is a rare specimen—a doll whose head is marked with the crossed swords of the Meissen factory. (The name Dresden is sometimes applied to the products of the Meissen factory.) She has a bun at the neck, and the form of her shoulders is so beautiful that one almost imagines one can see the delicate bones under her skin.

The late "Mother" Clear, whose California doll hospital was celebrated, said that among the many dolls that came to her, she had seen only one marked Meissen head. The mark on this head shows that it was made after 1832.

Her body, with china arms and legs, as well as her dress and undergarments, is ca. 1839–40. Her pink cotton dress has a low-cut, boat-shaped neckline.

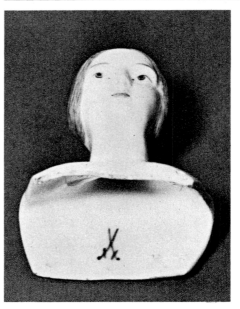

39 Two Jointed Woodens; *ca.* 1840; 7" high

With their special, primitive charm, the old jointed woodens have a peculiar appeal for many collectors. These two, being in the privacy of their boudoir, can reveal the interesting manner in which they are jointed. The doll standing is all wooden; the other, a rarer type, has head, arms, and legs of porcelain of that pinkish glow known as pink lustre. The wooden head has a thin coating of gesso which was applied before it was painted. This one's black hair is arranged in a bun at the neck, as is her porcelain-headed sister's.

The Biedermeier furniture, made in Germany around 1840, with its printed gilt decorations applied firmly and forever to paper over wood to resemble stenciling, is of a type made in endless variety for several generations.

40 Swedish Possibility; *ca.* 1840; 5½" high

When this early pink lustre lady turns her back on us, it is possible to see the wonderful tortoiseshell comb in her black hair. Her hairdo, which she wears parted in the middle and looping up from under her ears, terminates in braids which form a flat and imposing coronet.

There is an interesting possibility that this dignified personage is from Sweden—an early head from the Rörstrand factory (see Plate 108). Mr. Thor, a retired foreman whom the factory queried on behalf of the author, believes that the glaze might be the one used on Rörstrand heads and that the red "R" (underglaze) inside the head is very like the factory's mark.

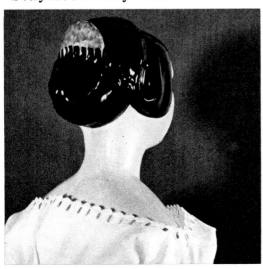

41 Two Shell Dolls; *ca.* 1840; 6¼" high

These two dolls are even less alike than two snow-flakes, but both are shell dolls and both are from ca. 1840. One is Dutch and the other French, and one can easily tell which is which!

The Parisienne has a papier-mâché head, arms and legs of wood, and undoubtedly a wooden body too, though that cannot be verified for the shells. She wears a skirt and shawl of light-weight fabric encrusted with tiny shells in lovely sub-dued shades of pink and beige, and over the skirt an apron covered with even smaller shells—all exquisitely designed and executed.

The Dutch doll is of wood in one piece, with no legs. The shells, light and dark, have been applied directly to the wood. The head is nicely painted, but rather crude.

One suspects that these may have been long-ago souvenirs from some seaside town.

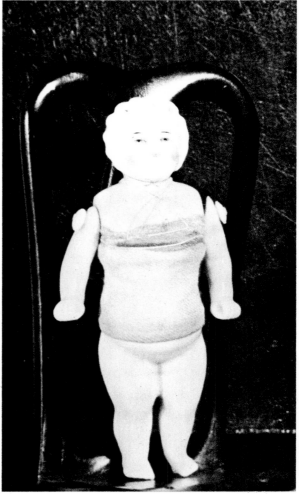

42 Cry Baby; mid-nineteenth century; 5" high

This baby appears to be a Frozen Charlotte till she is undressed; then one discovers that she has been "sawed in half" for the insertion of a squeak-box. Her arms, attached with porcelain buttons, are also non-frozen.

43 Papier-Mâché Head; *ca.* **1840;**
    4½″ high

With a center part and a bun at the neck, molded with her head, this papier-mâché with painted eyes is from ca. 1840. Papier-mâché was used for doll heads as early as 1810 in Sonneberg, and somewhat later in England and the United States.

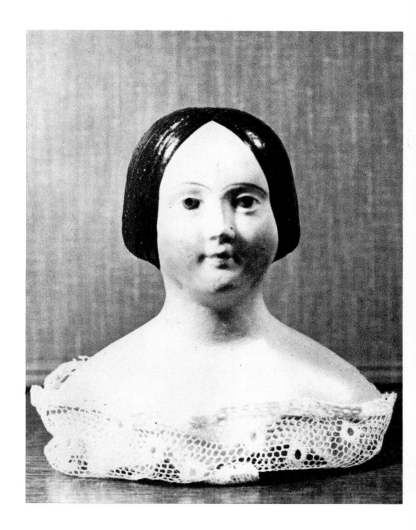

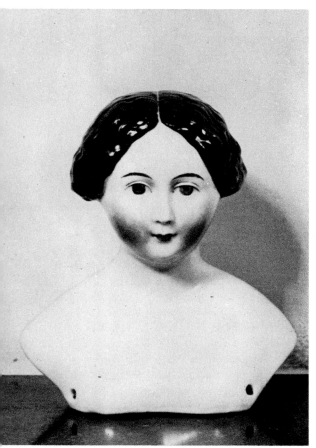

44 Lisbeth, a Pink Lustre; **1840–50;**
    4½″ high

This unusual head of pink lustre is from between 1840–50, perhaps closer to 1850 since her hair is not quite straight but has a moderate wave. Her coloring is lovely—the red of her cheeks has a color of its own—very soft and interesting. Her blue eyeballs protrude slightly, making her gaze a candid one.

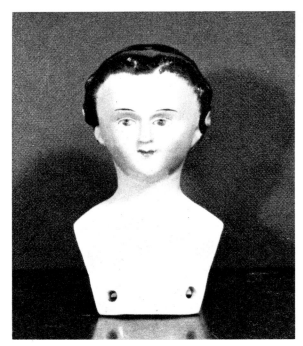

45 Rosamunde with Flowers; *ca.* 1840; 4″ high

This rare pink lustre head has simply beautiful color. The flowers Rosamunde wears in her hair, a different cluster on either side, are of the most delicate pastels. The shoulder piece is very narrow, and we have never seen another so formed. The very flat bun above the neck is typical of 1840, or else this most unusual head would be suspected of an earlier origin.

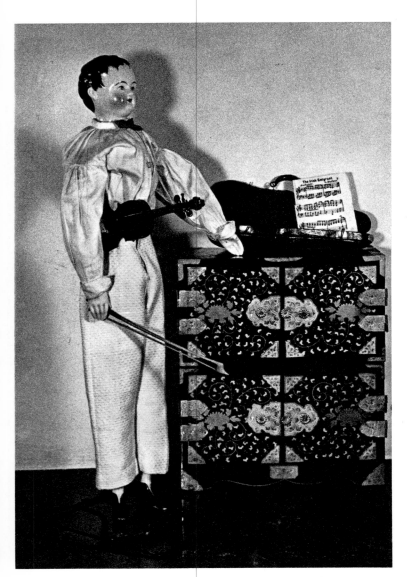

46 Violinist; *ca.* 1840; 19½″ high

Here is a doll and a violin; the author is not sure which is the more interesting. The young man has a history. He was given in 1840 to a little girl by a daughter of the Danish King Frederick VI. (The happy recipient was born in 1833.) He wears his original trousers and shirt, both beautifully made, and has a linen body, china arms and legs, and painted-on shoes without heels.

Although it did not come with him, his lovely little violin appears to be from approximately the same period and is a detailed replica of a real one. Its case is six and one-half inches long and lined with red velvet. The violin comes from Poland where it was obviously made with skill, care, and love.

The 1850's

47 A Bit of Fun; *ca.* 1850; 5½″

This sweet and funny wooden, ca. 1850, is a very practical joke. Although she herself is only one and a half inches high, she is rather imposing when she is seen, as she is here, in her white blouse and lovely green silk skirt. She is then all of five and a half inches. Despite her diminutive size, however, she has a bun at the neck, and her arms and legs are present, though small.

The two metal chairs, of the same period as Miss Fun, are French.

48 Ball; *ca.* **1850; (tallest doll) 14″ high**

Beneath the sparkling crystal chandelier, a stately company in elegant finery prepares to dance a polka. Gentlemen may seem in short supply, but the ladies are lucky to have even one partner since, as all collectors know, male dolls are not readily come by. Perhaps this is why this one's rather inappropriate costume of brown velvet jacket, white shirt, and brown trousers is tolerated upon this formal occasion. His partner is most suitably gowned in her original dress of white batiste with silk sash and matching trim in the soft red shade often to be seen on a doll from ca. 1850. Her undergarments are meticulous, her blouse has tiny pleats, and her fan is feathered.

The small blonde Parian is of a type called "Alice in Wonderland." Her arms and legs, as well as her head, are Parian, and her dress is cotton. Modeled on the illustrations by Tenniel, she is later than the other dolls, having been made soon after Lewis Carroll's classic appeared in 1865.

Chic in her black-figured white voile gown and black gloves, another member of the company (left foreground) is further distinguished by an interesting coiffure in which her long dark curls are drawn back to the nape of her neck.

Behind her is a doll of particular interest. Her porcelain head and shoulders, which include a fancy molded yoke and tie, surmount a body also unusual with its jointed cloth and papier-mâché hips, squeak-box, and wooden legs. Her boots are gaily painted on.

49 Two China Sisters; *ca.* 1850; 18½″ high

Twins, except for their china heads, these well-bred young ladies from Zealand belonged to two sisters born in 1844 and 1847 who, we may assume, were given their dolls in the early 1850's.

The head of the doll at right is a "Jenny Lind," so-called after the much-loved singer. The other has a hairdo with hair fluffed out at the sides and braids starting below the ears and joining in a bun at the neck. Both dolls have linen bodies and wooden arms.

Their dresses are of a woolen fabric, blue-green with stripes of brown and beige, and their exquisitely-made undergarments include underpants of the open type with legs joined only by the waistband. Both dolls have hand-knitted stockings, but Augusta still wears her black shoes with bands criss-crossed about her legs, while Vilhelmine has a pair of "new" shoes—new long, long ago. The sisters appear to be identically clad, but there is a small surprise: one has a pocket in her skirt containing a tiny handkerchief.

Pictured on the tole tray above the desk is an old Danish castle.

50 China Bonnet Doll; *ca.* 1850;
    12½" high

Since bonnet dolls are more easily found in bisque and are rare in china, this proper lady with her blue china bonnet and yellow china bow with delicately-colored molded flowers at either side is of special interest. One hunts for a Meissen or Dresden mark, but the fact that no mark has been found does not detract from her quality.

This doll also is of interest because of the prominence of her crinoline. Beneath her flounced white organza dress, she wears three skirts stiffened to give as much width as possible.

51 Early Baby Doll; 1851; 13¾"

This baby is very early, as she is from 1851, and that means something when one is a baby doll! Nearly all dolls till about 1880 were adults, and it is most unusual to see a baby doll dating earlier than the 'eighties. However, a similar doll was exhibited at the Great Exhibition in London in 1851, and this one's claim to the same year of birth is unmistakable. Her head, shoulders, arms, lower body, and legs are of papier-mâché and wood. Her mid-section is of linen and contains a squeak-box. She has dark glass eyes without pupils. Her hair, which has been painted on with very light strokes in a pale grayish tone, is faded and nearly invisible.

52 Emil; *ca.* 1850; 13" high

This boy was a nice surprise. Early one morning the postman rang and brought this doll as a present from an unknown person who had heard about the owner's "preoccupation." Male dolls, of course, are rare; among approximately four hundred dolls, the author has only twenty-five. If an undressed male comes along, finding clothes is practically hopeless, it being almost impossible to locate old ones for masculine dolls. Therefore, since Emil not only arrived in interesting clothes but also brought another blouse and apron along with him, he was a lovely present indeed.

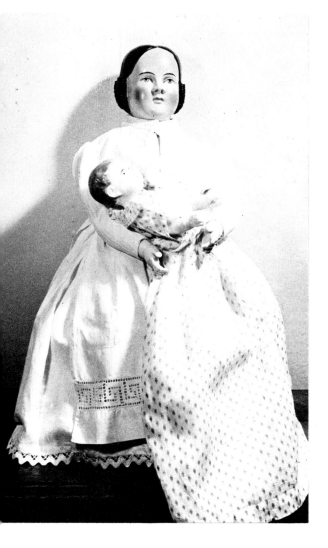

53 Juliane and Baby; 1850–60; 26" high

This nurse, who is clad in a clean white dress and apron and sits with a baby in her lap, is a real "personality." Her interesting porcelain head is a little coarser and heavier (and grayer) than one usually sees. Vertical black curls surround her head, and she has blue eyes.

The baby is also unusual. A Frozen-Charlotte type, she is of pink lustre and has golden hair. Her cotton dress, like herself, is ca. 1850–60.

54 Boy's Head; *ca.* 1850; 7½" high

This boy's head from about 1850 awaits a body and clothes. He'll wait through all eternity, one fears. But he's a nice boy with wind-blown black hair and blue eyes. It is interesting to note that all black-haired porcelain dolls have blue eyes.

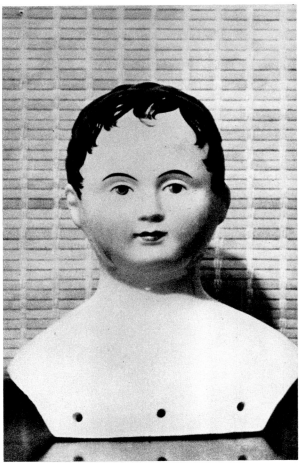

55 Wooden Doll; *ca.* 1850; 11½" high

As cross-eyed as a Siamese cat, this wooden lady can bend her elderly joints at shoulder and hip, elbow, and knee. She was found in London in her green velvet over lace with fringed pantalettes, which are probably contemporary. The bow on her bonnet is of a soft red often seen around 1850, her probable date of birth.

Color Plate 4: Martinique Doll; *ca.* 1850; 19″ high

This sweet and funny creature is all of brown leather, with a nicely formed and proportioned body with bosom. Her hair is, of course, black, but only a bit of it can be seen under her permanent turban.

Her dress of blue-patterned white cotton was surely made in Martinique. This is curiously "hiked up" in front which, judging from one very like it in the Louvre, is to enable her to carry a baby. The Louvre doll has a shawl tied about her hip with a child further supported by this arrangement of her dress.

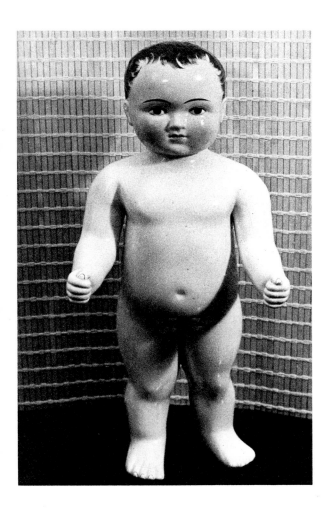

56 "Frozen Charley"; *ca.* 1850; 16″ high

This big fellow is the largest specimen of his type we have ever heard of, standing sixteen inches from his toes to the top of his black molded hair. We shall consider him the champion till someone writes and tells us of a larger "Frozen Charley." We prefer to concoct this term, since the traditional Frozen Charlotte is inappropriate in gender and the German word "steif" (for rigid) is not well known.

Even though he is, like most of the penny dolls, one solid porcelain figure without a joint to his name, he was hardly, as his tiny counterparts were, a penny doll. He has brown eyes with pink lustre on his head and neck.

57 Gabriele with Tiara; *ca.* 1850; 12½″

One needn't notice the glasses in her hand to know that this elegant personage, ca. 1850, is coming from the opera. Her golden tiara, molded onto her fine porcelain head, and her gold earrings are to the manner (literally) born, and we know that this grand dame has never washed a doll dish in her life.

Her crinoline dress, of red-printed cotton, has a true hooped skirt. Her arms and legs are, like her head, of porcelain, her body is of cotton, and her black painted-on shoes have no heels.

58 Shoemaker's Workshop; *ca.* 1850–80

Through the courtesy of one of those convenient anachronisms frequently present in doll establishments, we visit a shoemaker's workshop ca. 1850–60 with shoes ca. 1850–80. The shoemaker's tools are on his workbench, a roll of leather for new shoes stands against the wall, and in the boxes on the bench are heels and other items for repairing shoes or boots. Wooden lasts may be seen at the right and, on the chair, a nearly-finished shoe.

At the left, a pair of high shoes with laces ca. 1870 stand in front of leather boots ca. 1880. The wooden shoes at the right, wonderfully made (and no tourist souvenir), belong to the Berlin doll (Plate 35) and are about a hundred years old. To their left is a pair of saffian boots ca. 1875. A pair of red velvet boots without heels which unfortunately is almost hiden (right rear) has minutely inscribed under one sole "Tante Elise, September, 1852" (see Color Plate 5). Footwear was without heels until about 1860.

Dolls before 1840 nearly all have shoes painted on, some of them with laces criss-crossed up to the knee and ending in a bow. Small shoes with a buckle are occasionally found on small dolls ca. 1830, but these are fastened to the doll so that they may not be removed and photographed.

59 China with Glass Eyes; 1850's; 15″

A china doll with inset glass eyes is rare and interesting in any case, but this one may well be one of the earliest of its kind to be made in France.

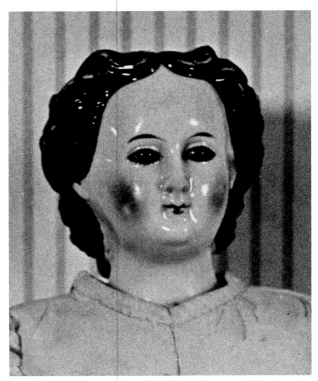

Her head appears to be of the type advertised by Blampoix Senior of Paris who, in 1855, took out a patent for the application of glass or enamel eyes to porcelain dolls. Although it appears to resemble the doll which illustrates the Blampoix mark in Elizabeth Coleman's book *(Dolls, Makers and Marks)*, we have learned, through the courtesy of Mrs. Dorothy Coleman, that the latter head has enameled eyes, and there appear to be slight variations in the head itself. The mouth on the Colemans' doll is larger, though Mrs. Coleman feels this may be a matter of the painting. The neck of their doll appears longer, and judging from the front view, so are her curls which are down to her shoulders. However, even though the dolls are evidently not from the same mold, their similarity suggests that they are of the same period.

Neither the doll's dress nor her wooden arms and legs are particularly interesting, but the doll and her glass eyes are indeed.

The 1860's

60 Parian with Feathered Coiffure;
ca. 1865; 16½" high

This proud personage has two feathers molded into her rare Parian head. Traces of gold and silver indicate that these were once of shimmering lustre. Two braids which frame her face coil flat in back, and a curl cascades down her neck.

This lady's clothes, though contemporary, did not originate with her, but her owner takes pride in her ermine muff with its tiny black tails, light blue lining, and tassels.

61 Drawing Room; *ca.* 1860; 15½″ high

It is plain that the daughters in this family group take after their porcelain father rather than their Parian mother who is an unusual member of that aristocratic family with her inset glass eyes. Her elegant coiffure, drawn back with curls at her neck, is entwined with golden beads and caught with a black band. She has a kid body and so has her husband who should not be in his fine drawing room in shirt sleeves (but we like our dolls in their original clothes, and his jacket, if he ever had one, is missing).

That the daughter in the black taffeta jacket is from 1860 is proclaimed not only by her hair (vertical curls and center part) but also by her china boots which, like those of all well-shod dolls of this type of about 1860, have no heels. The younger daughter appears to be an adopted child of mixed parentage, and even of mixed generations inasmuch as her linen body with its old painted wooden arms and legs is considerably earlier than her head of around 1880.

The mahogany handmade furniture is from the Virgin Islands, circa 1860. The wine bottles, of approximately the same date, are Dutch, and the grandfather clock is English—and it runs.

62 China with Net; *ca.* 1860; 5½″ high

This lovely and unusual black china head has, in the style of many a woman of fashion of about 1860, a net on her hair. This one, fastened with a band which ends in tassels at either side of her face, is knotted in the bow visible at the top of her head. The two curls reaching her shoulders and the "brushlines" of the coiffure are also of interest.

63 Ball-Headed Jo; *ca.* 1860; 16″ high

This attractive lady has a china head *and* a (hair) wig. Usually, of course, china heads have painted-on headdresses, but there are some ball heads among china dolls. Such an egg-shaped head has no hole in its top in which the wig is set, but has instead a black dot to indicate where the wig was to be fastened. (A ball head recently acquired by the writer has a "part"— a slit where the hair could be set in.) Some collectors believe these heads to be French. In a number of books they are described as Biedermeier, but that term implies an earlier date than this collector would assign to them. Having seen no ball head in clothes from before 1850 and having acquired all three such heads in her collection from their orginal families who judged them to be from 1860 to 1870, she inclines towards 1850–60 as reasonably accurate.

Jo has a cloth body and arms and legs of china. She has painted-on boots with low heels, indicating that she was made after 1860 since dolls' china shoes and boots had no heels before that time. Her dress is of printed cotton, and her blue bonnet, with flowers and tulle framing her face, is most becoming.

64 Victoria in Wax; *ca.* 1865; 15″ high

It seems quite possible that this imposing personage is meant to resemble Queen Victoria. English and made of wax with a linen body and beautifully fashioned wax arms and legs, she is much like dolls made by the Montanaris in London from mid-century to the 1880's. Her hair, set into her head with a hot needle two or three hairs at a time, is crowned with a tiara of silver threads and ribbons. This elegance is matched by her pink silk polonaise over a ruffled skirt of pink organza. Her be-feathered fan, on the chair, is of painted silk applied to light wood.

65 Doll with a Sentimental History; *ca.* 1875; 13″ high

Honest sentiment, alas, is not much in fashion these days, but for those of us who cannot resist it, the following letter which accompanied the purchase of this attractive porcelain is offered without comment. It came from an old farmer's widow on Fyn, just outside Hans Christian Andersen's birthplace, Odense.

"Dear Madam: Here is my little 'Sisse.' She has been much loved. My mother-in-law told me about her little daughter, born in 1868, who was fragile. To give her joy, they gave her Sisse, and she sewed her dresses and knitted her petticoat and constantly played with her. When she was twelve years old, she died with Sisse in her arms. Then the doll was put in the attic, where I found it. My daughter played with her and was so happy to have her that, as you will see, she mended some of her undergarments. When she was seventeen, she died, and I could not bear to see the doll any more. The museum would like to have it, but who then would keep her garments clean and mended? Therefore I want you to have it. Yours——"

66 Grandma as Baby Sitter; *ca.* 1860; 9½″ high

This funny little person, an old leather-headed doll with her grey hair sewn on, wears a red dress and white shawl.

The screen, covered with scrap pictures, is English and Victorian. The cradle is also nineteenth century.

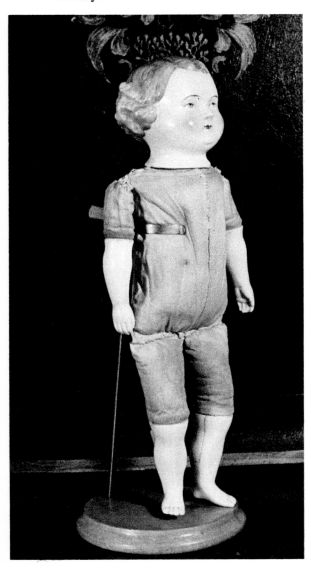

67 Dirck, a China Boy; *ca.* 1860; 12½″

Dirck is an unusual boy. From about 1860, he has head, arms, and legs of china, with a body of cotton. His head, with molded, light brown hair, is fastened in a rare fashion to his body. Although most china heads have a shoulder piece with holes for sewing them to the body, this doll's head is mounted on a rod which projects into the body and on which it can turn.

68 Regitze and Benedicte; *ca.* 1860; 10″ and 16″ high

One day Regitze and Benedicte, two sisters who are young friends of the writer's grandchildren, visited and admired the doll (the larger one) named after Regitze. When Benedicte expressed sorrow that no doll was named for her, the writer promised that the next doll added to her collection should be named Benedicte.

The next day a young man came to sell a doll and, by a remarkable coincidence, it was the same type of wax over papier-mâché as Regitze. This doll was smaller, but like Regitze, she had brown glass eyes, arms and legs with painted-on boots of the same material as her head, and a nice cotton dress. The two sisters, ca. 1860, therefore, are photographed together.

69 Superior Doll; *ca.* 1860; 24½″ high

Bought in Amsterdam and made in America, she crossed the ocean, as many dolls do, but not in the usual direction. It is unusual not only to find such a doll in Europe but also to discover one anywhere in such fine condition—and with half of her original label, in this case revealing that she is an "M and S Superior 2015."

She has painted eyes on her composition face, and her black hair, of course, is painted on too. An unusual detail is the underlining of the eyes, not applied in one stroke as is customary, but broken in this fashion:- - - -. Her linen body is not original. Her velvet cloak is worn over a dress of printed cotton.

70 Olympia; *ca.* 1860; 19½″ high

This composition-headed doll has a kidskin body like the one in **Plate 80**. Probably French, she has a ball head with a black spot on the crown, brown glass eyes, and straw teeth. (One can just see the teeth by peering into the narrow opening.)

Olympia's dress, from the late 'sixties, is of brown striped cotton. Her blue straw bonnet with bands and frills of tulle is of the same period.

71 Hostess from 1860; *ca.* 1860; 14″ high

The elegant creature presiding at her tea urn is an English wax head with a stuffed cotton body and wooden arms and legs. Her low boots without heels are painted on. She has lovely auburn hair, which she wears in vertical curls, also molded in wax. Her glass eyes are blue.

Her gown of pinkish silk with light brown trim is delicately fashioned and ends in a short train. There are frills and pearls and fringe in profusion, and this fashionable lady is wearing a handsome brooch.

She is evidently a collector of doll heads!

72 Joan and Her Wardrobe; *ca.* 1860; 20½" high

This woman from the late 'sixties came with a nice wardrobe consisting of: a pink cotton dress, a light flower-printed dress, a red cotton dress, a white ball dress, a pink dress with black lace, a black silk shawl with white tulle and a pink bow, a green hooded shawl, two bonnets, and two aprons. And one of her undergarments was a tournure, a knitted bustle with room for a little cushion. When she wore that under her dress, she got a little extra warmth!

Her head, arms, and legs are of papier-mâché with a thin layer of wax, and her stockings and boots are painted on. She has a cotton body with a squeak-box.

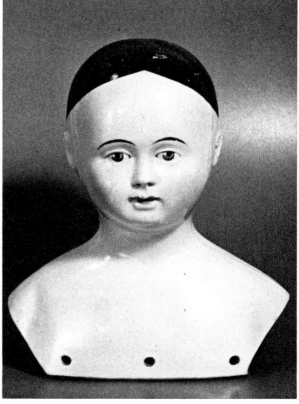

73 Unusual Ball Head; *ca.* 1860; 7½" high

This ball head is unusual for several reasons. Of pink lustre with a sweet expression, she has the usual black spot on her head to show where her wig should be fastened, but this is so large that it has almost the character of a hairdo itself! Perhaps this is not surprising inasmuch as her head is remarkably large, being all of seven and a half inches. One can only hope that it is not these characteristics which have turned her head—for her head *is* turned slightly—another unusual feature.

The 1870's

74 Herborg; *ca.* 1870; 23″ high

A nice young girl being photographed—that is why she looks so stiff! One recognizes the style from old pictures of great-grandmother. A black-painted braid surrounds her china head. Her kidskin body is one of the quite stiff ones; she cannot be made to sit. She is ca. 1870, younger than her white voile dress with its red figure which is from the 'sixties.

75 Drawing Room; *ca.* 1870; 16″ high

Three of these French dolls are marked. The lady at the left, who wears a light blue wool dress beautifully fashioned with *plissé* and pleats, is marked "F.G." on her left shoulder. Her body, including hands and legs, is kid, her hands are made with separate fingers, and she has a swivel neck.

The doll near the fireplace, wearing red satin covered with black tulle and lace with red silk bows descending her small train, is believed to be a Bru. Also swivel-headed, she has two marks: on her neck, "B o S," and on her kid body, "Mon. ALPH. GIROUX." She is pictured and described more fully in Plate 76.

The seated doll came to Denmark in the year 1873 with a basket of flowers on her arm. Her dress is of red and black checked cotton, and she wears mittens. She, too, has an "F.G." mark on her left shoulder and a swivel neck.

The doll whose back is turned is unmarked, and she has a stationary head. She wears a plaid cotton dress, typically 1870.

On the writing desk are two marked silver items from Amsterdam: a coffee pot, 1755, and a water jug, 1757.

76 Ninon, a Bru; *ca.* 1870; 12″ high

This French lady of fashion, who may also be seen in Plate 75, is believed to be one of the Bru dolls so eagerly sought by collectors. This one, who is swivel-headed, has two marks: on her neck, "B o S," and on her kid body, "Mon. ALPH. GIROUX, 13 Boulevard des Capusines, Paris." She came to her owner with a nice little trunk full of clothing, hats, shoes, boots, umbrella, ermine muff and cap, fan, and many other small articles. A label inside the trunk lid reads: "Maison AL-PHONSE GIROUX successeurs DUVINAGE & HARINKOUCK." A hat box inside the trunk has its own label: "BOISSIER Á PARIS." (Elizabeth Coleman, in her recent book *Dolls, Makers and Marks*, reveals that F. Duvinage and Harinkouck succeeded Alphonse Giroux between 1864 and 1867.)

Therefore this doll came with an unusual amount of documentation—of much interest to doll scholars. Although Bru dolls usually are marked "BRU" with the letters in a vertical position on the body, Mrs. St. George in *The Dolls of Yesterday* describes a wooden-body Bru in her own collection with an incised "B 2 S" "across the back on the bottom of the chest." Mrs. St. George does not give the size, but presumably this "B o S" is smaller. Elizabeth Coleman considers "B o S," "B 2 S," and others in the series undocumented marks, but the dolls so marked appear to have all the characteristics of a Bru.

The gown that Ninon is wearing is of red satin beneath black tulle and lace. A procession of red silk bows descends her short train.

77 French Stockinet Doll; *ca.* 1870; 17″ high

She is a stockinet doll—a reference to her body which is of wood with a cover of stockinet, an elastic knitted fabric. Her head which turns is not unusual (and no less beautiful for that reason), but such a body is relatively rare. It is pictured in Plate 80. Fine undergarments are beneath her lovely handmade dress.

78 "French Fashion"; *ca.* 1870; 19″ high

Here is a lovely lady from Paris, a wooden-bodied "French fashion" with reddish curls and a bisque face with fine coloring that sets off her creamy white silk and reddish brown velvet princess-style dress. Like all French dolls, she has beautiful eyes which shine like stars. Her remarkably jointed wooden body may be seen in Plate 80.

This lady's smart little hat is adorned with flowers in matching colors, and her boots of morocco leather are high-heeled.

Color Plate 5: F. G. Doll; *ca.* 1875; 22½″

This doll was bought in Paris, and under one of her tiny red velvet boots (without heels) is written in an infinitesimal hand, "Tante Elise, Sept. 1852." So we must assume that the boots are of that date, but the doll is not, being undeniably a generation later—*ca.* 1875.

She has a swivel neck, blue glass eyes, pierced ears, flaxen wig, and a very nice kid body which can be seen in Plate 80. Her hands are exquisitely made; her feet are also unusual, with each toe defined. The well-known "F. G." mark is on this lady's left shoulder.

Although many questions remain, Elizabeth Coleman, in her valuable book, has done a great deal to sort the confusion surrounding this mark. Gesland, a Parisian doll-maker in business beginning in the 'sixties, and Greffier, who was making dolls in the early days of the Jumeau Company, are always considered when F. G. marks are mentioned, but Gaultier (sometimes spelled Gautier), who founded his Paris firm in 1860, seems the most probable maker of the doll pictured. The Coleman book, which is scholarly and does not jump to conclusions, says: "It seems likely that the French bisque doll heads marked F. G. were made by Gaultier, but it is also possible they were made for Gesland." Miss Coleman gives much evidence to support this view. Luella Hart, in *The Spinning Wheel*, August, 1957 and August, 1960, offered pioneer research about these and other French doll-makers.

The dress of this doll, which obviously originated with her, establishes her age. Of dark pink satin trimmed with beautiful French lace, this lovely gown has no binding sewn inside the skirt to keep it tight around the knees—a style which came in *ca.* 1875 and which such a fashionable lady would have followed.

79 Another French Lady; *ca.* 1870
13½″ high

This French doll wears her original dress and hat from the years around 1868–70. Her dress features an overskirt and is banded in red, and her straw hat is trimmed with a blue band and flowers.

Her head swivels, and her body of kidskin is similar to the one at left in Plate 80. An "O" is incised in each shoulder.

80 Three Bodies; 1870–75; 22½″ high

Our heading would make a fine title for a murder mystery. Instead we offer you three French fashion dolls with bodies of different kinds—one of wood, one of wood and stockinet, and one of kidskin. The stockinet, center, and the wooden, right, are especially attractive. The fine kidskin lady, left, looks a little bent and tired, though she is no older than the others. But this sort of body will, as time goes on, get sawdust in the gussets and become impossible to straighten.

The wooden doll is the most agile. She is moveable in fourteen places—all the usual ones and in the middle of her upper arms and in the middle of her thighs as well. The stockinet body is also easily moved and is particularly well-proportioned and attractive.

These dolls, dressed, are more fully described in (left to right) Color Plate 5, Plates 77, 78, and 79.

81 Patrician Lady; *ca.* 1870; 15¾″ high

This demure and lovely head, with rare downcast eyes, came to light at the death of its elderly owner; the delicate and beautiful arms and hands had been put in a teacup! Her new owner attempted to discover the age and origin of this remarkable doll who looks down as no doll ever has before, but positive information has been elusive. With her lovely coloring—her hair is very, very light, and she has a white bow on top of her head—she seems to fit most readily into the period around 1870, and luckily, a gown of that time, pink gingham with little lace frills, has been found for her.

She stands before a chest of drawers, a Buddha head, and candlesticks with glass hurricane shades —all from the Far East, whence she may have got her facial expression.

Color Plate 6: Fine Lady; *ca.* 1875;
   5″ high

This unusual Parian has blue glass eyes, pierced ears, and a remarkable coiffure, its honey-colored strands attractively defined and crowned with a comb. Her elaborate collar and yoke, its charming pattern further embellished with frills and bows (all in pink, blue, black, and gold) molded, of course, in the Parian, is most elaborate.

82 Two Jumeaux Automata; late 1870's; 16" high, height of box: 3"

On the backs of the heads of this disarming pair, under their wigs, a celebrated mark may be discerned: "DÉPOSÉ TÊTE JUMEAU Bte SGDG 3."

These mechanical dolls contain music boxes, and when their keys are wound, they play their mandolins and turn their heads from side to side while a sweet melody issues from the boxes on which they stand. The machinery in the boxes is marked "40," a numeral without meaning for the writer, but possibly a clue for future historians.

Both the brown-eyed Troubadour, who wears red velvet, and his blue-eyed lady, who wears pink and beige satin, are in their original clothes. The sleeves of their playing arms are well-worn from years of strumming.

83 Amager Doll; *ca.* 1870; 17″ high

This parian aristocrat comes from Amager, and if you come to Copenhagen by air, so do you! (The airport has been built on this little island connected by three bridges to Copenhagen.)

About two hundred years ago the Danish king invited some Dutch farmers to move to Amager and grow vegetables much needed in Copenhagen. Some of the great-great grandchildren of those farmers still live there, and once in a while, when they attend a feast or wedding, they dress in the charming embroidered costumes of their ancestors. This lovely Parian with her ball head, glass eyes, pierced ears, original wig, and fine kid body shows exactly how they look on these festive occasions. She wears her original dress and undergarments, and even her stockings are embroidered.

84 The Empress Elizabeth; *ca.* 1870; 8½″ high

This doll has a history. A letter from the London dealer who sold her states that she was given originally to a Countess Zymi by Elizabeth, consort of Francis Joseph, Emperor of Austria and King of Hungary. (This Bavarian noblewoman was born in 1837 and, alas, murdered in 1898.) This noble doll is, quite obviously, a "sewing companion." Although she has her original red-banded white muslin dress beneath, her charming outer dress of multicolored gauze delicately edged with a tiny frill probably held needles and pins. At the back there is a sort of pocket, undoubtedly for scissors.

She has a Eugenie headdress and is probably from ca. 1870.

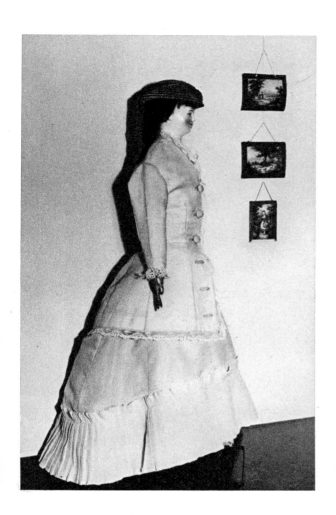

85 Charlotte; *ca.* 1870; 22″ high

This china ball head with wig has a kidskin body and is nicely dressed. She wears a well-tailored jacket and skirt of cream-colored wool. Her jacket is trimmed in Valenciennes lace, and her skirt has a wide *plissé* at the bottom.

Her fingers are free, and on her feet she wears funny old boots, not as smart as might be expected from the rest of her costume. Her straw hat has a blue band with streamers at the back.

86 Rare Parian; *ca.* 1875; 6¾″ high

Griselda not only has black hair, rare in a Parian, but also another unusual feature: a medallion molded in the Parian, hanging from a blue molded strand. Her elaborate hairdo, with many puffs at the back, is crowned with a blue band. She has pierced ears and blue eyes.

By a curious coincidence, the author has a twin to this doll, identical except for its lacking the medallion. Inside the twin's shoulder, inscribed with ink, is "1875," suggesting that Griselda's date is the same.

87 Ball-Headed Parian; *ca.* 1870; 22″ high

This patrician Parian, bought in England, came into the world without a hair on her ball-shaped head and is obliged to wear a wig. Her head is solid, having no opening in the top such as later heads usually have. Nearly all bisque heads of later make are hollowed out, with cork inserted for attaching the wig, a practice initiated after 1860 to lighten the head as well as the duty which was levied on weight at that time. Since French doll-makers imported many heads from Germany, such weight was an item, but it might be noted that doll heads not made for export continued to be made with solid heads.

This Parian's body is kid, and she wears a cotton-print dress and earrings of old silver in her pierced ears.

88 Welsh Lady; *ca.* 1870; 13" high

When the lady in the substantial piece of millinery was purchased, she was described as a "Welsh lady coming from the market." Her milk jug over one arm and her basket filled with tiny cakes over the other help substantiate this claim. Under that extraordinary hat, she wears a cap of real lace. Under *that*, with its yards of narrow black silk looped round and round, she not only bears a striking resemblance to a Grenadier Guard, but seems, with her knitting pinned to her glazed calico dress, well-equipped for the most extraordinary adventure.

Her china head is of a type made through the 'seventies and 'eighties.

89 The Diligence; mid-nineteenth century; 22" high

This English stage coach, ca. 1860, was obviously in Her Majesty's service, "VR" for Victoria Regina being painted with a flourish on its sides. In mellow shades of yellow and brown, this diligence has luggage on top and seats behind as well as within. (In 1795, a journey from London to Norwich cost £2 10s for two inside places and 16s for one outside.) It is probable that outside seats were more of a bargain in every way; four to six people jamming the tiny space within was possibly unbearable in those nonfragrant days.

Both coachman and lady passenger are ca. 1870. The latter is a jointed wooden, and the coachman, a bonnet doll with his hat molded to his Parian head, has Parian arms and legs and a cloth body. The horses are of wood covered with camel hair.

90 Finissima; *ca.* 1876; 15¾" high

This name means "the last one." That was what this collector meant it to be—the final one in her collection. So rare and delicate and fine and with a beautiful and well-preserved dress, she is a type of doll her proud owner had sought for a very long time and would now stop collecting. But did she?

The lovely head is of papier-mâché. The coiffure with numerous puffs and two curls falling down the shoulder is typical of the 1870's. But the date is more specifically stated; on her neck in ink is "1876".

Finissima's gray wool princess-style dress is embellished with turquoise silk. Her underskirt is also princess style, and all her undergarments are as perfect as her dress. They have never been washed, a tribute to the care with which their wearer has been preserved.

91 Kirsten; *ca.* 1870; 20" high

Her owner thinks so highly of this charming doll that she has named her Kirsten after one of her daughters. One of those light bisques which are close to fine Parian, this girl crowns the top of her blonde coiffure with a black bisque bow. She has bisque arms, but wooden legs amusingly painted with yellow stockings and black boots.

Jet earrings accent the black braid trim of her green wool dress, and tiny matching jet beads are sewn to the braid. The back of her shoulder is marked "S 10 H" inasmuch as she was made by Simon and Halbig, one of the best makers of German bisque doll heads.

The 1880's

92 Parting; *ca.* 1875–80; (tallest doll) 12″ high

The young daughter is going to leave her home, and her luggage stands ready to load on the pony cart. Her mother, her young sister, and two aunts are there to see her off, and even their pet donkey came along to say farewell. They are all from about 1870, except the aunt (right) who is a little old-fashioned (ca. 1860). Their ages may be judged by their headdresses—so much like that of Empress Eugenie.

  The mother, who looks wistful, has a Parian head with black hair (unusual in a Parian), with traces of gold remaining in the band around it. The animals are by Schoenhut, that celebrated maker of American dolls and toys who came from Germany and later, in 1872, opened his Philadelphia factory. These animals are from one of his famous circuses.

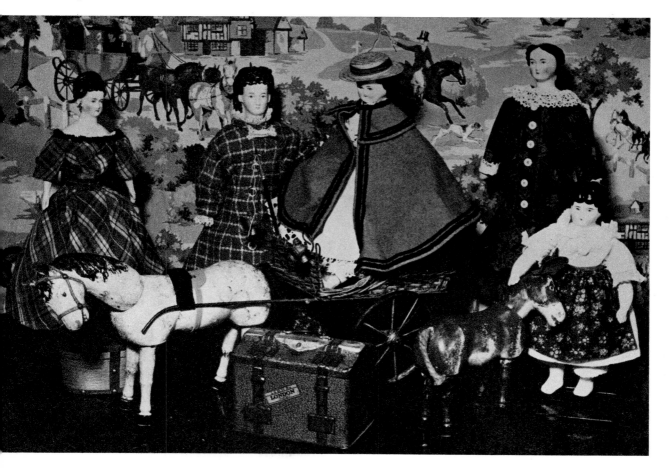

93 Bride from *ca.* 1880; 17″ high

Poor bride! We realize that she is unimportant, being a rather common blonde Parian, ca. 1880. It is her costume which is interesting, her lovely bridal gown of rather heavy cream-colored satin with a nice long train. All *plissé*, be-laced, and pleated within an inch of its hem, it is a model of a dress worn by a young lady in Denmark in 1880.

Photographed in her parent's house, she looks a bit wistful, as though she knows that somehow she is out-done both by her costume and by her surroundings.

94 Alexandra; *ca.* 1880; 5″ high

The writer has called her Alexandra because of her striking likeness to Denmark's beloved princess, later Queen of England. Her head is of bisque, very light in color, with hair in a stately arrangement upon her head that needs no crown. Since she was found in England, it is interesting—and curious—that her clear, glass eyes are brown. The story goes that because Queen Victoria had blue eyes, all the dolls sold in England during her reign were ordered with blue eyes, with brown-eyed dolls sold elsewhere in Europe.

95 Wax Daphne; *ca.* 1880; 17½″ high

This wax doll has a nice wig. A small tiara adorns her fine brunette braid. Her head, shoulders, arms, and legs are all of wax, and she has blue glass eyes.

Daphne's dress is of black velvet with satin front and numerous tiny buttons, some of which serve to lace her bodice. Her boots are painted on the wax and have a charming gilt paper edging around the tops.

96 Balthasar; *ca.* 1880; 7″ high

Because he appears to be one of the Three Holy Kings, this stately figure has been named Balthasar. Cradling the Christ child in his arms, he undoubtedly was part of a Christmas crib.

His velvet coat, embroidered with gold, may be seen beneath his mantle which is made from a French shawl. His armor is fashioned of tiny shimmering glass pearls which also sheathe his cardboard sword. His crown of crimson velvet is surmounted by beads and multi-colored glass pearls of larger size.

The beard is painted on his face, an addition to a conventional porcelain head of ca. 1880. The hairdo serves to date him; without it one might have thought him of somewhat earlier vintage.

The Christ child, a Frozen Charlotte, is simply clad in beige cotton with a hood and swathed in a red velvet shawl.

97 Child's Head; *ca.* 1880; 5″ high

This bisque child with brown glass eyes is German. Her molded light hair is short with deep waves, and her shoulder piece is marked "203/8" (a number which may be of use to future doll researchers). She has a sweet expression, and when one looks at her, one feels that she has a lovely soul!

98 Ball Headed Rasmine; *ca.* 1880; 16¾″ high

This interesting Parian with ball head and glass eyes has her original wig and a very fine blue woolen dress with lilac velvet banding. She really should wear her dress inside out to reveal the fine sewing which has gone into it. The lining and the numerous small bands necessitated by the bustle are exquisitely made. Rasmine has a kid body, Parian arms, a small golden tiara in her golden hair, and a nice little handmade handkerchief with real lace in her tournure.

99 Stinne; *ca.* 1880; 21½″ high

This lovely child has head, arms, and legs of bisque and a cloth body. Her wonderful blue glass eyes have a sweet expression, and her golden hair is, of course molded, on. She wears a bonnet, a fine white dress from the 'nineties, and white shoes and stockings.

A bell is incised between the numbers "131" and "9" on the back of her shoulder piece.

100 Klara; *ca.* 1880; 15¼″ high

This doll is included in tribute to the patience of children in 1888. A little Danish girl was given this doll in that year along with permission from her mother to take it out of the cupboard every Sunday to look at—not to play with. The little girl looked forward to this moment all week, and she kept her doll until her recent death at the age of eighty.

The doll, still in her box which is labeled, in Danish, "1/12 *dus. Dukke*" (1/12 doz. dolls), wears a red silk dress with lace and nice boots with high heels. Her hat is there too; it has not been used much since the doll has spent all her life indoors. Klara's shoulder piece is marked 167 4, a fact which isn't especially informative now but may be of use to future doll historians.

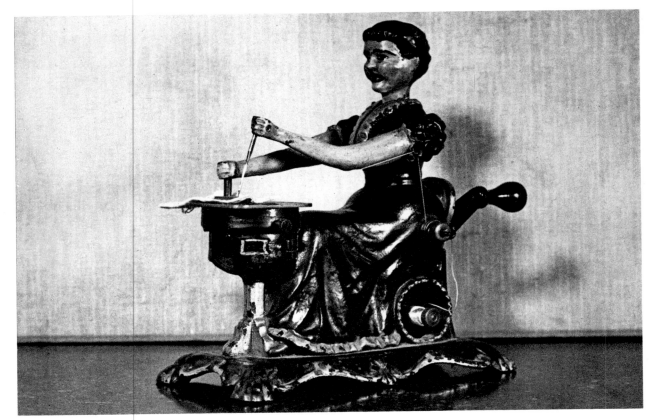

101 Sewing Machine Doll; *ca.* 1880;
7½″ high

It was irresistible to include this in a book about dolls, but it really isn't one. It is a sewing machine and most intriguing. What's more, it still can sew, turning out doll dresses with the nicest chain stitches. When the handle at the rear is turned, the figure's left hand goes up and down, sewing, while the right hand gently guides the fabric.

One wonders if it can be American. It has no marks but bears a resemblance to certain American iron toys from around 1880.

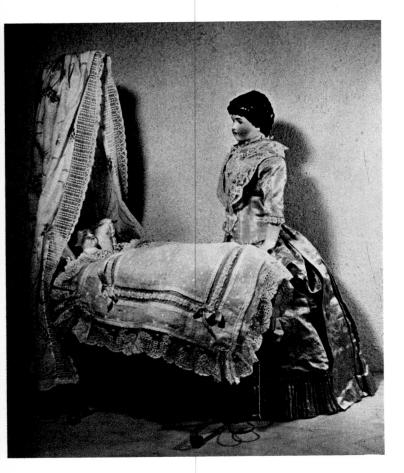

102 Good Night Visit; *ca.* 1880;
23″ high

The china-headed mother, who gazes adoringly at her china-headed child, has an unusual hairdo of bangs beneath a braid which surrounds her head. Her dress is quite wonderful: heavy silk of light blue in the fashion of 1883 with bustle and *plissé* trim. Just as interesting inside as out, it is lined, with stays ribbing the bodice and with wires and bands to keep the bustle in place.

The metal cradle is also of interest. It may be rocked comfortably from a chair by operating the foot pedal attached to its base.

After 1889

103 Two-Faced Doll; *ca.* 1890; 11″ high

Towards the end of the nineteenth century, small girls began to demand more and more of their dolls. Some of these could walk and some talk, but this one can turn her head and achieve a new expression. She has two faces, and a frilled bonnet hides the face "not in use." One face is smiling and the other near tears. The head is of bisque—surely German—with glass eyes and is fastened in the usual manner to a composition body. (Earlier china and papier-mâché heads have shoulders with holes for sewing them to the body, but later heads end at the neck and are fastened from within the body.) The small metal ring which looks like a watch stem at the top of her head is, of course, what turns her head.

This doll was dressed as an infant at the time of her purchase, but under the baby dress she wore her original white dress as a chemise!

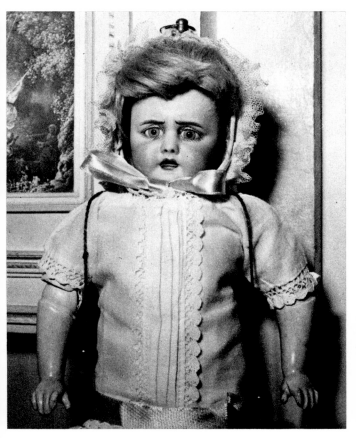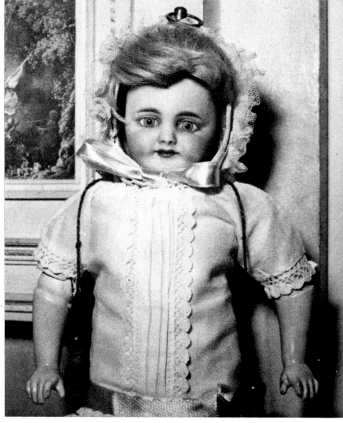

104 Lady from 1890; 22″ high

This china-headed lady from the 'nineties with her black hair and lovely red cheeks is one of surprisingly few—considering the number made—that survive with original costume. It is perhaps of interest to note that "things" were not held in such high esteem after the 'sixties and 'seventies. Everything was more easily made, doll dresses found in shops were no longer done by hand, and mass-produced doll heads were considerably cheaper—a condition which has continued to spread until the present when our stockings are thrown away when we find a hole in them. Therefore it is relatively rare to find dresses from 1870–90, and especially ladies' dresses. Until 1880 most dolls were dressed as adults, and thereafter mostly as children. As that was a new idea, nearly everyone wanted a child doll, so that ladies' dresses of this later period are now quite scarce. This lady's dress is of white batiste with little frills of Valenciennes lace on the bodice. Her sash is red.

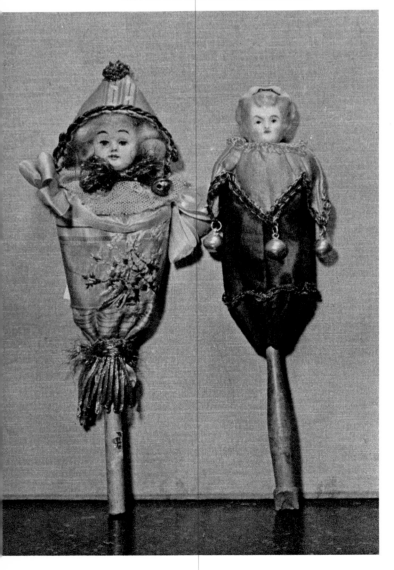

105 Two Rattle Dolls; *ca.* 1900; 11″ high

This curious pair dates from around 1900. They rattle when swung about, and their little bells tinkle. The one to the left has a bisque head, and the other a china one. The latter has a whistle. Both dresses are of silk in shades of blue.

106 Lady with Hair-Do; *ca.* 1890; 22″
 high

From 1890, this lady has a very elaborate painted-on headdress. So much happens here that it would be difficult to describe! Her hair is piled high on her head with braids slung about here and there. One doubts that such a coiffure could be achieved with real hair.

She is clad as an adult—relatively rare for this period (see Plate 104)—in a woolen dress with leg o' mutton sleeves, a narrow waist, and trumpet skirt. She has a cloth body and china arms.

107 Little Girl at Play; *ca.* 1890; 18¾″
 high

This brown-eyed, brown-haired child has wax-over-papier-mâché head, arms, and legs. Brown boots with tiny buttons are painted on her feet, and she wears a red velvet dress with a nice pink pinafore over her linen body. She is surrounded by some of her most cherished possessions—her doll, her donkey, and her school copybooks and pencil case.

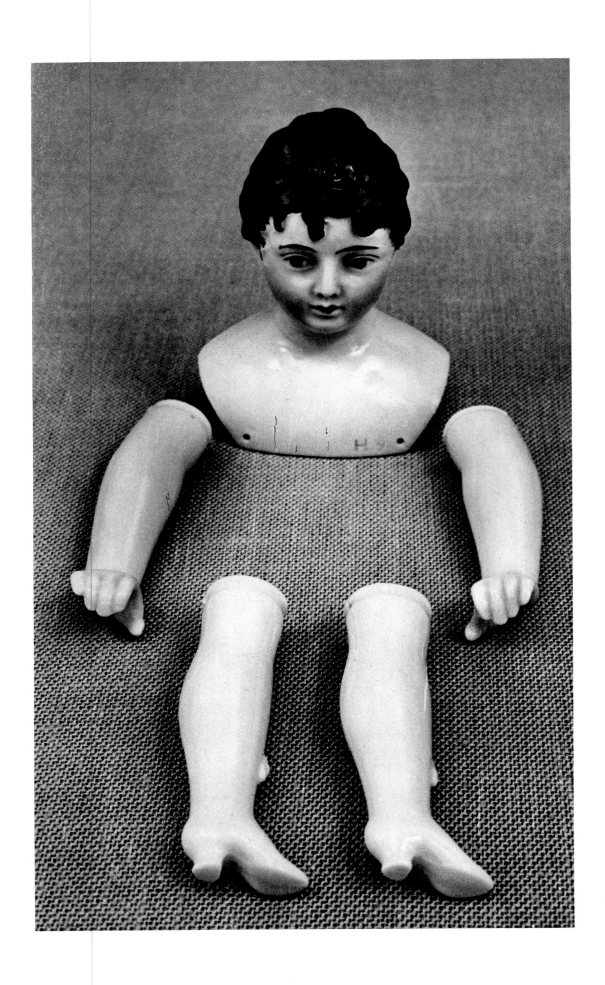

108 Swedish Discovery; *ca.* 1900; 5″ high

This doll, discovered just as this manuscript was being completed, is quite a find. Until this one appeared on the scene, no doll had been found which could, with certainty, be identified as having been made in the Rörstrand factory. (A possible Rörstrand head may be seen in Plate 40.)

Rörstrand, the foremost Swedish porcelain factory, which has been in operation since 1726, made doll heads, arms, and legs. This fact was disclosed in 1960 when a museum publication in Lund, Sweden quoted an 1868 Rörstrand catalogue. Ever since that time, the writer had attempted in vain to identify positively two china heads of her own as products of the Rörstrand factory. Then, just in time for inclusion here, came word from the factory that while unpacking some collections, a doll head, arms, and legs had been found and would we like a picture!

It is also through the great kindness of Miss Brita Malmström of the Rörstrand factory that when this picture arrived, it was accompanied by information given by a retired foreman of the plaster model section, Mr. Thor, whom the factory sought out. According to Mr. Thor, this head was made around 1900, as it was "poured," while the earlier ones were hand-modeled. The incised "4" which may be seen on the shoulder piece is a reference, of course, to the size of the head (five sizes were made), and the "H," to the fact that the factory had reached model H in its line of heads. Within are the letters "ML" which Mr. Thor believes are the initials of one Mathine Langseth who worked as a painter. The painting of doll heads, according to Mr. Thor, was usually done by young girls beginning their education as painters. The legs, modeled with boots on, are, as the picture shows, unpainted. It is believed that the factory made dolls till around 1900.

109 Auto Tour, 1905; size: 14″ × 15½″

This irresistible vehicle is of red-painted metal with rubber tires. A spare is on the running-board where the gas container also has its place. In addition to the headlights, there are two smaller lights below the windshield, and there is even a license plate printed by a young hand showing that the car has its home in Copenhagen.

The fine lady has ostrich feathers in her hat. She and her companion are both from a doll house.

110 Straw Doll; *ca.* 1917; 10″ high

Never has a little girl been without her doll.
Even in the darkest moments, there must be
time for play. This sad little creature is a German
doll made in the final years of the first World War.
She consists of a bit of newspaper filled with
straw and held in place by her "costume" which
consists of some small bits of cloth (four different
materials) for a dress—and a picture for her face.

Glossary of Doll Terms

Ball Head: A round porcelain head without wig or molded hair-do.

Biedermeier: From a German style of furniture, 1815–48. Term is also applied to dolls of approximately this period.

Bisque: Unglazed porcelain.

Bonnet Doll: Bisque, porcelain, or occasionally wax dolls with molded hats or bonnets.

Bru: A French doll-making family of the second half of the nineteenth-century. Although Bru dolls were made in various materials, the sought after Brus today are characterized by large, luminous glass eyes set into bisque heads of fine quality. Bru doll patents were taken out as early as 1867.

Composition: A mixture with a base usually of sawdust, paper, or flour in combination with paste or glue.

Frozen Charlotte: Non-jointed doll of china or bisque.

Gesso: A pasty composition such as plaster of Paris applied to wooden doll heads to facilitate painting and heighten detail.

Jumeau: Fine French dolls produced by a factory founded in 1843 and continuing operations throughout most of the nineteenth century. These high quality bisques, with glass eyes of a beauty unmistakable to knowing collectors and dressed in finely detailed costumes, are avidly sought by collectors.

Lustre: A subtle pink and lustrous coloration to be found on certain porcelain nineteenth-century dolls of superior quality.

Papier-Mâché: A composition made from paper of a porous texture, saturated, usually with a mixture of flour and glue. Used for doll heads perhaps as early as 1810.

Parian: A fine bisque, pure white, with no color added before firing.

Penny Doll: Small dolls costing a penny. The earliest were the "penny woodens," and there were some waxes (probably rare, because few survived). More traditionally known as penny dolls are the small Frozen Charlottes of later vintage. Later still were wire-jointed stone-bisques.

Plissé: Gathered or plaited fabric.

Polonaise: A garment consisting of a waist and drapery in one piece worn over a separate skirt.

S. F. B. J.: French abbreviation for Société Française de Fabrication de Bébés et Jouets (an association of French doll makers established in 1899).

Stone-Bisque: Coarse type of unglazed clay.

Terra Cotta: Red biscuit earthenware varying in color according to firing, from pink to purple-red.

Valenciennes: A type of fine bobbin lace formerly made in Valenciennes, France and, since the early nineteenth-century, made largely in Belgium.

Wax Dolls: Various types of thick wax heads or papier-mâché heads dipped in wax. Types vary over a long span of years.

PART TWO

DOLL HOUSES & SHOPS

by Flora Gill Jacobs

The Family in front of the South Jersey House

Introduction

A small gilt object, an inch and a half long, with a threaded screw and a purple velvet top is among the items shown on the following pages. If it were to appear in a handful of jewelry, it might be mistaken for an earring, an unastonishing article to which it bears a striking resemblance.

But it is not an earring. It is a miniature sewing clamp with a pincushion top, an object rare even in full-size, and the only one the writer has personally seen or even heard of. It may do as well as any small treasure can to epitomize a theory of which this volume is an elaboration: After years of collecting the items illustrated on the following pages, the collector begins to believe that practically everything which has ever been made in full-size has also been made in miniature. As the accompanying photographs may suggest, a noticeable amount of time has been spent in attempting to prove this hypothesis.

When early in one's collecting days, the wall telephone, complete with crank and ringing bell, first hove into view, the theorist thought the ultimate support of her theory had been reached. But since then, the wall 'phone has appeared and reappeared, with one bell on top, or with two, or with other variations, and the collector has gone on to greater wonders, each unique, surely, in its survival if not in its existence, until the next *pièce de résistance* was found: the gilded lead medicine chest with labeled bottles of miniscule pills and spirits and packaged rolls of wadding, the pocket-watch holder, both wall and dresser model, and then—one's current ultimate—the sewing clamp alluded to above.

Mr. George Speaight, in his delightful book about the English toy theatre, muses upon the wonders of collecting: "One hundred separate pictures or books, scattered among the houses and shops of the earth, are only one hundred separate and divided facets of a complete jewel; but gathered together (if they are intelligently chosen), they can combine to illuminate each other and together form a complete consensus of, for instance, a school of painting, or the development of a social fashion. This is a Collection. It is something greater than the sum of the individual articles of which it is composed. . . ."

This admirable defense of those of us who, like the jackdaw, must collect is, for doll house collectors, the gilt on the gingerbread. We're glad to have it, but our case, like the gingerbread, is good without it! In the doll house, it is possible to see reflected not only the development of *a* social fashion, but of many fashions, social and domestic. In the doll shop, stable, and schoolroom, our microcosm, with its portraits of daily life, is further extended. The connotations and ramifications are wide and astonishing.

Travelers have traditionally roamed the earth gazing at old houses, palaces, and castles, some containing their original furnishings or ones believed to be similar. George Washington's card table is in the parlor at Mt. Vernon, and many of the other important furnishings remain, but the authenticity of unimportant ones is in doubt, making the picture as incomplete as Gilbert Stuart's celebrated portrait of the mansion's owner. When a good old doll house is found intact, the brooms are still in a corner of the kitchen, the leg o'mutton is on the sideboard, and even Nanny's petticoat is showing—as true a portrait of daily life as ever Vermeer painted.

In *A History of Dolls' Houses,* one attempted to describe four centuries of such portraits in words. In the present volume, one hopes to offer a more limited, but possibly more vivid segment in pictures. This segment, covering approximately a century, is bounded by the limits of a quite representative collection assembled during a period of nearly two decades. Since pre-Victorian doll houses and related items are largely in museums and what remains to be collected is primarily Victorian—early, mid, and late—plus those few ornamental years knows as Edwardian, all collectors are likely to be confronted by similar boundaries. They may even, as the writer has, broaden them to admit the period right up to and including the 1920's, slipping in an item such as a crystal set or a hair dryer when it is especially evocative of, for instance, the 'twenties. (Anyone who doubts that this period of time has become a distinctive era may be converted by certain passages of this summary.)

With the return of the Victorian era to grace, a preponderance of Victorian doll houses seems appropriate in a book which, it is hoped, will intrigue non-collectors as well as collectors.

The latter, however, are becoming multitudinous. Although the creating and/or furnishing of doll houses by adults is a pursuit well-known for at least four centuries, in 1945, when the author's collection was begun, doll house collectors were still a relatively limited group. Those of us who inquired in antique shops for these toys were likely to receive surprised or patronizing looks from proprietors who could not conceive of a market for such ephemera. But things, as the saying goes, have changed. Now seekers of these wares—"miniatures," as so many dealers refer to doll house items in confusing opposition to the small portraits which for generations had exclusive use of the term—find them hard to come by for a different reason: dealers have had them and promptly sold them! Many a collector has been met by the same phrase: "Just last week I had. . ." and the dealer names some treasure for which one has been longing.

Of all such treasures, the hardest to come by is the furnished house. The sad economic fact exists that dealers can profit more handsomely by selling the contents piecemeal. Dealers, of course, are in business; the rest of us can only regret that they are dispersing history. Occasionally a fully-furnished house escapes—to a museum or even to a private collector. It is hoped that such printed pleadings as this will free a few more.

The contents of the dismantled house are scattered to a variety of collections, whose collectors may be classified under a multitude of categories. Some furnish individual rooms, some "do" houses, and some towns. Not long ago, a Missouri dealer mentioned that she had three "castle collectors." These, it seemed, (possibly inspired by Colleen Moore's castle or merely by a more personal vision of a dream castle?) sought such things as swords, crests, and wall hangings fashioned from old petit point or tapestry purses.

Such improvisations are the province of still another category of collectors; those who make things out of other things, as opposed to those of us who merely collect. Collecting at its best, as Mr. Speaight so aptly suggests, is a creative pursuit, but the improvisers and the builders seem more wholeheartedly entitled to be called creative than those of us who merely "collect and arrange."

The latter group may be further compartmentalized. Those of us who acquire only antique furnishings which we attempt to place in houses of the proper period may tend to be a bit snobbish about collectors who mix antique pieces with reproductions. We may even feel something close to actual pain when we hear of the members of that insensitive caste who take antique pieces and "re-do" them.

The collection pictured is, of course, limited almost entirely to antique doll house furnishings, but even within this category further refinements are possible. Items made for doll houses are preferred by most of us, but inevitably ones made for other purposes have found their way into doll rooms: cabinet pieces, party favors, salesmen's samples. Although adults always have been in the picture, children, after all, have been the true interior decorators of doll houses, and if offered a Dutch silver spinning wheel or an ivory settee for their dolls, would they likely have refused? The candy box in the shape of a grand piano, moreover, may have an inexpensive realism superior to either of these. This collector, for instance, would resist the silver (unless interpreted realistically in a tea set or some other item appropriate to the material) but is quite partial to Austrian bronze (see Plate 191), an artistically painted ware from which the potted plant, for one example, often has made a superb doll house accessory. In this collection, the ivory settee would be scorned, but the candy-box piano welcomed, especially if it interprets with fidelity, as several examples do (Plate 192, extreme left), both the object itself and the spirit of its era.

Many an antique dealer appears to be mystified by just what is and what is not a salesman's sample. Although these tend to be larger in scale than doll house pieces and are relatively rarer, many dealers of otherwise impeccable judgment infer almost automatically that any well-made miniature furnishing must be a salesman's sample, and innumerable doll house furnishings have been incorrectly described to purchasers as such. It must be confessed that the writer of these words was tempted till recently to suspect a small brass bed (Plate 169) of such origin. In perfect scale and style, with a small, removeable wire spring of similar perfection, it seemed a plausible candidate for salesman's sampleship until a drawing of this very bed was noted in F. A. O. Schwarz' 1913 Christmas Review as "Brass, 6 inches @$1.25" and "8 inches $1.75." (This could also be had in enamel at lower prices.)

Neither the value of catalogues to collectors nor their scarcity need be belabored here, although one might take further note of this regrettable rarity. In years of seeking catalogues as well as doll houses, this collector has unearthed a pathetic few to illustrate doll houses, doll furnishings, or shops, even in libraries and museums. A recent catalogue compilation was purchased with high hopes, and its most promising leads investigated—with little result.

Shortly before this manuscript was completed, Mrs. Faurholt found a German toy catalogue, ca. 1848, in the Copenhagen Museum. Unfortunately, the title page of this treasure is missing, but what remains is an unusually complete record, not only of toys of the era, but necessarily of the shops and the rooms which they accurately reflect and of the furnishings and costumes of the dolls—and therefore the people—who inhabited such premises, both miniature and full-sized. A dramatic example of the worth of such catalogues appeared in the form of the remarkable coincidence of the presence in this long-ago catalogue of an illustration of a butcher shop in the author's collection (Plate 200). The original shop sign, "Bull Butcher," on the front of the shop had implied a British origin, but the catalogue, complete with these two English words, reversed the author's well-established conviction. Some of the catalogue items are labeled in German and some in English, the latter ready in the last detail, this makes clear, for export. A number of these catalogue plates showing dolls and doll houses are reproduced in the two sections of this book, and one regrets that it is not possible for more of these, especially in their delicate colors, to be reproduced.

It is unfortunate that toy firms have preserved so few of their catalogues, but one cannot go further in this brief introduction without alluding to those which the celebrated New York toy store, F. A. O. Schwarz, has assembled (and one's gratitude for access to these.) Part of a page from their 1913 Christmas Review showing doll house furniture and a doll house is shown in Figure 1, and other illustrations from this useful brochure are scattered throughout the text. Although the firm's well-known history in New York goes back to the 1860's and the remaining catalogues in their possession, with one exception, do not begin until a well-illustrated Christmas circular of 1910, studying even these relatively recent ones has been most informative.

From a collector's point of view, this study has also been full of surprises, some of them depressing. The late Frank L. Ball, the celebrated Cambridge toy collector and dealer, concurred with a plaint of the writer that catalogues tend to reveal the youth of toys one had thought older. It is, of course, true that a successful set of doll house furniture was often continued, with very little change, for a number of years. Some of the items in Schwarz's 1913 catalogue, such as the brass bed which has been described, were also shown in the 1910 circular. One was longing to see earlier Schwarz catalogues to know how old such items might be, as well as how new, when an 1894 Schwarz catalogue was found which provided a dramatic example. The kitchen shown in Plate 157 (detail), which is taken from the 1913 catalogue and was to be seen in succeeding ones up to 1918, was identically presented in 1894, establishing at least a twenty-four-year span for this particular toy.

Some pieces which had been considered pre-World War I have been discovered in catalogues astonishingly modern. Iron toy stoves with imitation stove pipes and names such as "Eagle" and "Star," stoves one tends to associate with the Victorians, may be seen in "Our Drummer" for 1932. Similarly, though somewhat earlier, in a Selchow & Righter catalogue of 1920–21 are iron scales with weights, also of a genre one might have thought of in late nineteenth century terms. Perhaps these iron items were temptingly inexpensive to continue when the molds were available, just as they appear to be tempting to reproduce today when the original molds can be found.

The search for dates and sources will continue. One anecdote may serve to elaborate upon the hazards and rewards of hunting for the materials themselves.

Shown in Figure 2 is a davenport in light polished wood, its three small drawers on one side and door on the other being identical to the drawers and door of the exceedingly interesting, more sizeable desk along side. The latter is part of a remarkable bit of toy history largely destroyed, alas, but of considerable interest still. According to the Pennsylvania dealer from whom it was purchased, the larger desk was found with

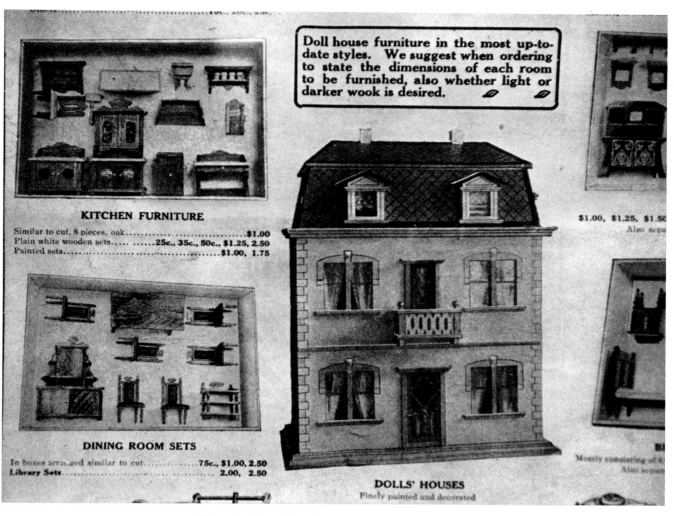

KITCHEN FURNITURE

Similar to cut, 8 pieces, oak................$1.00
Plain white wooden sets...... ....25c., 35c., 50c., $1.25, 2.50
Painted sets..$1.00, 1.75

Doll house furniture in the most up-to-
date styles. We suggest when ordering
to state the dimensions of each room
to be furnished, also whether light or
darker wook is desired.

$1.00, $1.25, $1.50
Also separa

DINING ROOM SETS

In boxes arranged similar to cut.................75c., $1.00, 2.50
Library Sets............................. .... 2.00, 2.50

DOLLS' HOUSES
Finely painted and decorated

Mostly consisting of
Also separa

Figure I: *From F. A. O. Schwarz' 1913 Catalogue*

Figure II: *Three related desks*

several desks in other styles in a traveling toy salesman's sample kit, and with an astonishing addition: a glass-globed lamp, each in a different style (student, etc.) to accompany each style of desk! The kit bore the printed legend: This is our Fall line for 1871. Although the dealer attempted to sell the unit (for a sizeable sum) for two years, he finally felt obliged to take this bit of history apart and dispose of it piecemeal. The writer bought the last remaining desk (the lamps, the dealer said, having sold in a rush) and attempted, of course, to learn the name of the manufacturer. Unfortunately, the dealer remembered only that the firm's location was New York State.

There is a footnote to this sad little tale which reveals how curious the bypaths of collecting can be. Two days after buying this desk in one Pennsylvania county, the writer bought an almost identical desk in another county. But the second desk was less "almost identical" than it first appeared to be; although the style was the same, the quality was plainly inferior—the reddish-stained wood had not as fine a finish, and the appealing side drawers and door of the 1871 desk were absent entirely. This desk was stamped GERMANY on the bottom, suggesting that it was at least a generation later than the other, and yet its measurements and its metal knobs were identical. After these three desks were photographed, an even more elaborate specimen, obviously of the finer, polished wood series, was found in New Jersey and may be seen in Color Plate 11.

This strange set of similarities and discrepancies suggested to their owner that the 1871 "manufacturer" was probably an importer rather than a maker and that the two desks were both from the same German source with, as is so often the case in miniature furnishings, much of the quality subtracted from the later version.

If the German stamp hadn't implied a later dating, there would, of course, have been the possibility that the same manufacturer had made his later pieces in several qualities. A revealing old toy catalogue advertised many grades of doll house furniture at graduated prices: in "oval boxes," "common red varnished" and, better, "red polished." Furniture in "square boxes" came in even greater variety: "red polished, fine polished, extra fine polished, and extra fine with marble top tables, bureaus and washstands and with chairs and sofas covered in silk." (This catalogue by Stirn & Lyon, 20 Park Place, New York City is, unfortunately, not dated.)

Because it is difficult to be explicit in describing certain types of doll house furniture, it is helpful to see how their manufacturers have gone about it in these old catalogues. Perhaps the most sought-after Victorian doll house furniture has been the imitation rosewood type with gilt trim (hand-painted on the earlier pieces and printed on the later ones). Alice Winchester, in *The Antiques Book,* pictures a Greek Revival center table made in New York ca. 1830 and observes that, "The fine stenciled decoration as a substitute for ormolu mounts is an American invention." This full-sized improvisation obviously was rivaled abroad by the same thought in miniature. An antique dealer in Germany, from whom some of this furniture was purchased, described it as Biedermeier, and the pieces were indeed of that simplicity of line one associates with the style. Other later furniture of this genre often has the more ebullient curves and flourishes of the later Victorian, and perhaps Mrs. Greene[4] is wise in her choice of the term "Doll's Duncan Phyfe," though it seems somewhat cumbersome.

[4] *English Dolls' Houses.*

In this connection, one reads with interest in an 1886 issue of *The Youth's Companion* of a "Doll's Toy Parlor Set" comprising "nine pieces including a real marble top table, sofa, six chairs, and a bureau. It is *imitation ebony and gold* upholstered in figured cretonne and is much handsomer than cut shows." The italics are our own, underlining a contemporary description of this attractive furniture. Although Frances Lichten[5] points out that rosewood was the most favored of the exotic new types of lumber which replaced "Good old English oak" and imported mahogany and that "in mid-Victorian days, no well-to-do home was without its parlor suite and piano of this dark, red-brown wood," she also notes that ebony from the East Indies was a favorite for pianos and piano keys.

One's choice of other descriptives must also be somewhat arbitrary. It might be necessary, almost, to assay the doll house metal to determine which is pewter, which Britannia, which lead. Most amateurishly, this non-metallurgist has employed a sort of rule-of-thumb: if the piece is early and tough, that is, with the strength of pewter, she is likely to risk calling it pewter. The filigree pieces which have been made for generations and which nearly bend if one looks at them are usually designated "soft lead." Tin, as a rule, is mercifully unmistakable. Another metal plentifully found in Victorian doll houses, and of a glistening appeal, is the embossed brass which Miss Gertrude Sappington, whose magnificent "Gay Nineties Mansion" is known to many collectors, insists should be called ormolu. Since brass is most commonly thought of as a heavier metal than these lightweight but lavishly embossed pieces suggest, her word may indeed be useful.

In every collecting area, especially a relatively youthful one such as doll houses and their furnishings, small confusions of this sort are likely to exist. There is also the problem of scale. The purist will not admit in a doll house scaled an inch to a foot any item which is even triflingly out of line in either direction. Here may be a question of whether one is furnishing model rooms or a doll house. Again it might be noted that doll houses traditionally have been furnished by children, who are not as finicking about such matters as adults. One fortunate enough to find a doll house with its original furnishings should be reluctant to remove anything at all. Toy kitchens seem often to be supplied with pieces enormously out of scale, a fact which diminishes their charm not a whit. (The antique toy department of F. A. O. Schwarz had for sale at one point a set of French filigree furniture in which the grand piano and the mantel clock, still sewn in their original box, were about the same size.) When assembling a doll house, a good eye, not a measure, seems the better judge. Furnishings of somewhat divergent scales may co-exist under the same small roof if they are in different rooms and, with care, even in the same room. Since identical doll house pieces frequently were made in several scales, sometimes a "set" is found in which a bed, for instance, might swallow up the matching chest. The original buyer's choice was erroneous; one has the alternative of putting asunder what was joined together generations before or of letting the pieces remain together in the certainty of their mutual age and aura.

Such matters as these are primarily of interest to the collector. In assembling this volume, we have hoped also to intrigue the general reader—or, at least, the general

---

[5] *Decorative Arts of Victoria's Era*, Scribner's New York, 1950.

reader who, like the author, is in love with the atmosphere of the past. The assembled pictures are an attempt to show how, even in miniature, that past may be vividly presented, in some ways, perhaps, more completely than in full-size. Without taking a step or turning one's head, one may look into a doll house room and perceive this atmosphere and absorb, in the bargain, a great deal of information about the period which created it.

Being fondest of discovering the pieces which most thoroughly illustrate atmosphere and which recall bygone practices and customs, this collector has attempted, wherever possible, to include a bit of full-sized history along with the miniature, offering approximate, and sometimes specific, dates and circumstances in connection with an invention or trend. (It is astonishing to discover how quickly upon the heels of, say, the full-sized vacuum cleaner, the toy version followed.)

Because of technical difficulties, it has been necessary to omit a few categories which might have been included. Mirrors are difficult to photograph, and even though every sort may be found in the collection pictured—pier, cheval, shaving, and less specific varieties—no attempt was made to impose this category upon the photographer. But in this reference, it seems pertinent to note that these are multitudinously available. One had also hoped to have a selection of "soft goods": doll house towels (often initialed and fringed), tablecloths, napkins, carpets, and draperies. Fabrics, among the most challenging items to reproduce in miniature, have often been reproduced with remarkable success, but they are even more challenging to photograph.

Also omitted are the few items as yet unfound in miniature which are bound to turn up some day. One longs, for instance, to discover a causeuse or ottoman, that most Victorian of furnishings, which sat roundly in the elegant Victorian drawing-room, often with a potted palm at dead center to shelter those seated circularly beneath it. The Wardian case, that glass receptacle so similar in appearance to the aquarium, but an indoor accommodation for plants rather than fish, has also eluded this collector, so far. . . .

Such things have been sought. Sometimes things unsought, but even more curious, have appeared. Not pictured, for instance, is a perfect model of a Victorian coffin (six inches long) given by an elderly British friend who said it had been "dug up" in Surrey. One wonders if it had been the non-final resting place of a pet bird. Somberly, indeed morbidly, it exists, but since it adds to the complete picture, one is grateful.

One had hoped to have a category of doll house dolls—especially those small bisque people found in Victorian houses in their original impeccable dress—the ladies and gentlemen and the maids, the butlers complete with bisque sideburns and towel on arm, the little boys in their sailor suits, the grandmothers in their caps. These small people, instead, lend their imperturbable bisque façades to a cross-section of the pictures, supplemented, as an extra dividend, by a catalogue illustration (see Figure 3) of six adults and a baby.

It was a temptation to include an appendix with some of the marvelous doll houses which have appeared since *A History of Dolls' Houses* was first published in 1953. There is the Hayes house, made for young Fanny Hayes when her father was in the White House. There is the superb town house, built for New York City's Brett children between 1830 and 1840 and now at the Museum of the City of New York. There are several impressive private collections of houses and shops, including the small select few of Mrs. William Redd Mahoney of Oak Park, Illinois and the enormous sprawling melange of Mrs. Homer Strong of Rochester, New York. There is the fine collection at the Shelburne Museum in Vermont and the equally fine one in Mary Merritt's small, superb Museum of Dolls and Toys at Douglassville, Pennsylvania.

But the temptation had to be resisted. The history was a project grounded almost entirely in research, mingling the scattered records of a subject not previously assembled between the covers of a book. It seemed imperative to admit photographs of as many important doll houses as possible and to limit the groups of chairs and bric-a-brac and the close-ups of chandeliers and other minutiae which one longed to offer in profusion. Since the present volume attempts to fulfill this latter longing and to make room for as many telling details as possible, an appendix seems expendable.

Figure III

However expendable an appendix may be, that paragraph known as acknowledgments is not. It would be impossible to conclude without giving thanks to Mrs. Henry Erath of F.A.O. Schwarz who made catalogues available, to Dr. Elisabeth Wolffhardt of Munich, Germany who has been helpful with many details, especially those pertaining to kitchens, to Mr. C. R. Harper who patiently took the bulk of the frequently complex photographs for the doll house section, and, especially to Mrs. Laura Treskow of London, England who, over a period of a number of years, found some of the major items in the collection pictured, thus making this book possible. There is also, as always, my husband, Ephraim Jacobs, who not only has read the words but, in the case of this project, has lent a cool head and an understanding heart to a writer beset by the complexities of a book combining a collaborator in Copenhagen and an editor in Tokyo.

Years ago, the author wrote a book for children in which various miniature objects were to illustrate certain aspects of domestic history. A sample picture (see Figure 4) shows three inkstands: an eighteenth-century porcelain holder with removable pots for ink and sand; an ornate mid-Victorian affair in ormolu with wells of ribbed glass and a matching ormolu roll blotter; and, from the 1920's, a stiff green metal stand with hinged pot and a "post office" pen the length of a straight pin cradled in its base. It is a procession not only of inkstands and of the writing customs of the eras these represent, but also of the styles of the eras—the materials that were used and the manner in which they were interpreted.

Figure IV

That book, for a very different audience, has never been published. It grew into the present album, which is offered without further preamble. . .

Flora Gill Jacobs
16 West Kirke Street
Chevy Chase, Maryland

List of Plates: Part Two

COLOR PLATES

BLACK & WHITE

I The Houses

111 Georgian Baby House; 41″ high

Eighteenth-century English toy houses, and even early nineteenth-century ones, were invariably called baby houses, and this one may be as early as 1760, A two-story house of the Adam period at the Manchester Art Gallery (England) has almost identical twelve-light windows, similarly arranged in threes, and there is a similar pitched roof with twin chimneys at the back.

Unfortunately the original door has been crudely replaced, and the original interior has fared little better, but the lovely taffy paint, found on so many English doll houses, and the handsome proportions of the façade are intact. Although no lock or catch guards the swinging front, whose original hinges have obviously been replaced, it fits perfectly, wonderfully unaffected by the extreme variations of many English winters and several Washington summers. Strips at the base of the house indicate that the traditional stand is missing. Such bases, which usually complement the architecture and sometimes are almost an integral part of it, are a feature of old English doll houses (Plates 115 & 116)

It is likely that only the shell is intact, with some fond parent having attempted a rather amateur-ish restoration of the interior a generation or more ago. (A clue to the age of these "improvements" may be found in the lower hall on a paper "molding" cut from a page of *The Bystander,* a British publication of relatively recent vintage.)

A great hall-style staircase with a Chinese Chippendale balustrade has been attempted in paste-board. Several steps meticulously made (the others are cut casually from one block) suggest that these survive from an original staircase, probably central and simpler in concept. There is also the possibility that there were originally no stairs or partitions, but instead the simple but frequently found arrangement of one room to a floor. Door openings have been crudely represented, and it is likely that all partitions are of recent origin. (A cardboard partition surrounding a staircase opening in the third floor has been removed by the present owner).

Because of the dubious nature of the interior, the partial furnishings which came with the house are also suspect; but only their association with this particular house is under suspicion. Some of them are unmistakably early and fine—the four poster bed with pineapple carving and gilding (shown in the detail picture) among them. This bed may well have been made by the same hand that fashioned the set of wheel-back windsor chairs with saddle seats which accompany a tavern-type table in the hall. This table and the chairs may have originally been in the kitchen, which is now too small to contain them.

A rather flimsy homemade kitchen dresser, a tin fireplace, and a few other built-in additions are unfortunate, but one can be grateful when such an ancient toy survives at all.

112 Georgian Surprise; 10″ high

This tiny Georgian domicile was offered as a doll house and accepted as a doll house. Its architectural qualifications are apparent, and it contains dolls as well as furniture. But these are forever invisible to the camera's eye, for the very reason which causes one to question the purpose of this charming curiosity—the small house is sealed! The fourth wall is not only present, but is inviolable; the windows and door are air-tight.

The single room inside is fully occupied by a (relatively) Gargantuan couple seated at a round table—the bearded gentleman in knee britches is reading, undoubtedly aloud, since the lady in her cap across from him appears to be listening. They, as well as the furniture, are of wood and delicately painted. A handsome stenciled wallpaper is at the rear wall, and floral papers are at the other three.

Perhaps this was meant to be a variation on the peep show, that popular seventeenth-and-eighteenth-century divertissement—this, a rather primitive interpretation without the complexities of perspective.

113 Early Victorian House (exterior); mid-nineteenth century; 41½″ high

When this house was sent from England, it was described as "Regency," but "Early Victorian" appears to be a more accurate designation. Although the exterior is a modest interpretation of certain Regency features, with flat roof, balustraded parapet, matching balustraded windows, and classical window cornices, it seems prudent at least to allude to "the last flicker of the great classic tradition of English architecture" which Osbert Lancaster (*Here of all Places,* Houghton Mifflin Co., Boston, 1958) calls "Kensington Italianate."

This might link the house with the 'forties and 'fifties when houses very similar to this one were built in multiplicity in Kensington, Paddington, and Belgravia. One possible clue to an earlier date are the Venetian blinds painted at the tops of the windows. Fashionable in the eighteenth century, their vogue began to wear off around 1840, at which time, according to Frances Lichten *(Decorative Art of Victoria's Era),* "Green, their usual color, was going out of fashion." These blinds are green, but, of course, they may have been painted on the windows by one not quick to follow style.

114 Early Victorian House (interior); mid-nineteenth century; 41½″ high

Whatever the date of the "Early Victorian" House, it seems to have been redecorated at mid-century. There are velvet lambrequins on the fireplaces (two of which are corner ones), and all the decorations appear to be of similar vintage. The smaller picture shown is a "before" picture of a house which was discouragingly grimy before restoration was begun, and the larger picture was taken after a beginning had been made.

The interior is so truly early Victorian that this period has seemed the logical one to restore. Someone had made an unfortunate beginning by painting the upper right-hand bedroom a brilliant yellow, forever obscuring the perfectly-scaled printed wallpaper which, in other patterns, still hangs somewhat faded but thoroughly evocative in three of the other rooms. Along with papers and draperies, many of the pictures and mirrors are still intact, and some furnishings came with the house, but one weeps for the rest, recently dispatched, it would seem, from what was obviously a thoroughly furnished residence. Still, one must be grateful; sixteen looking glasses remain—in seven different styles—including, in the drawing room, the oval pair from which the glass is missing but which boast pricket candleholders. One, a type we have not seen before, has a cloak hanger at either side of its base. These mirrors are supplemented by a variety of gaily lithographed pictures in metal frames, and the fact that all are in the fine clutter of their original positions (with tiny nails attesting to the locations of others) is especially appealing.

It was probably at the time that these were hung that the elevator was added. A heavy metal frame with a shelf, tucked behind a rear projecting wall, this resembles a dumb-waiter in style but an elevator in scale, and one hesitates to call it either. It is operable by a pulley attached to spools on the roof. The curious staircase, with fretwork balustrade and oddly-placed landing, also appears to be an addition.

Most interesting, whether it was added at the same time or earlier, is the black tin kitchen range, an unusual corner one like two of the fireplaces. Again like the fireplaces, this is a manufactured piece, including its blue criss-crossed white tin backing (to which a wooden superstructure has been added). It features a hinged oven door at either side of a central grate above which are embossed the words "The Model Bakery." A full-sized oven not unlike this appeared on the market at the end of the eighteenth century. The plate rack in its original position above the sink and the dresser with wire rails to hold the plates further embellish a kitchen with a distinct flavor.

115 English Victorian Gothic; early Victorian; 46″ high

As British a doll house as one would wish to see, this small early-Victorian Gothic is a modified castle, a thing of turrets, buttresses, battlements, and irrelevantly, chimney pots. Painted a soft red to resemble stone, with white trim, the small house is built to fit into its own stand, which, like those of many English baby and doll houses, matches the house and completes it. One must examine this stand carefully to see where it ends and the house begins.

When the door handle, on a spring latch which fastens the whole front, is turned, the two window sections swing open on either side of a fixed front door panel. Each of the four rooms has a mantelpiece with a built-in metal grate. These correspond to the chimney (a thing doll house fireplaces often fail to do) and may be seen from the side windows. By manner of their four-paned arrangement, the arched Gothic windows betray their Victorian origin.

116 English Victorian with Stand (exterior); *ca.* 1850; 61″ high

Perhaps the most traditional feature of the English dolls' house (and the English always use the "s'") is the stand on which it rests, usually, as in the case of this attractive specimen, an integral part of the architecture. The supports of this stand are carved to resemble stone. Realism has been carried further in the case of the coigning which has been applied in individual blocks.

The walls are painted a soft red divided into small bricks with a careful brush, and the "stone" base, coigning, lintels, and other trim are painted the lovely traditional taffy color so often found on such houses. Door panels and shutters are of an unusual grained wood. Scroll-cut oak ornamentation under the eaves is the Victorian touch on a house of otherwise almost Georgian simplicity.

117 English Victorian with Stand (interior); *ca.* 1850; 61″ high

Since it came with many of its original furnishings intact (a number of late Victorian additions have been replaced) and in excellent condition, this handsome house is of unusual interest.

The early, marbled, book-end paper which, discreet investigation reveals, originally covered the walls, is happily undisturbed in the hall. Nice old wallpapers, less carefully applied, have covered it in the other rooms. A true staircase with landing and balustrade dominates the hall, though two rows of tacks are all that remain of the stair carpet. Carefully handmade grates are built into the wooden chimneypieces (this is, after all, a British house), and these are filled, in proper scale, with genuine coal. It is curious that in a residence with so much careful architectural detail as this one, no provision is made for going from one room to another. A doll who happens to be in the hall may go upstairs or down, but no doors open into any of the rooms.

Several early dolls survived this indignity, including a nice peg-wooden cook with her original rust-sprigged cotton gown and commodious white apron. Three blonde bisque sisters with their mid-nineteenth-century flat hairdos and flat shoes have been supplemented by a bisque nanny with her equally mid-nineteenth-century sausage curls, her striped tan uniform, and her white cap.

A small sleigh bed, a chest with bone supports at either side of the three drawers, a corner what-not with four shelves, and, most interesting, a bookcase with double glass doors and "books" (Plate 163) are among the "rosewood" furnishings which came with the house. A banquet table with leaves, lavender-silk upholstered chairs, and a mirror-backed china cabinet of the same material have been added.

From across the channel, a French parlor set, in light wood with fancily-turned legs and rust silk upholstery and with embossed floral scraps glued to table tops and cabinet fronts, adds gaiety to the conservative surroundings. Among these pieces, which include chairs, sofa, parlor table, desk, and a corner cabinet with bow front, is a pier-type mirror with a plant stand below. (Only the shreds of the plants remain.)

A small marble-top table with metal dolphin legs (Plate 181) was one of the most unusual pieces found in this house. In the kitchen, an oval fish stew pan, the inevitable plate rack, and one of those nice, plain, straightforward cupboards with doors below and drawers and pigeon holes above (to be found in so many Victorian doll house kitchens) are among the original fittings.

118 English Cupboard House; early Victorian; 44″ high

Aside from a pitched roof and front windows for each of the six rooms, this English mid-nineteenth-century cupboard house has no architectural pretensions, but the proportions of the wide, deep rooms lend themselves ideally to furnishing.

Rather amateurish false doors, strangely placed as identical pairs at the rear of each room, flank the original metal fireplaces, each a different and attractive commercial model; and the wallpapers, carpets, one pair of lace curtains, and one chandelier (fortunately firmly attached to the ceiling) are also original.

A handsome taffy-colored print paper with harmonizing oil-cloth on the floor help to make the kitchen especially appealing. The exterior, incidentally, is also painted this warm taffy shade. The base was originally mounted on short legs with castors which have been unscrewed for convenience of display.

For the most part, furnishings from English mid-nineteenth-century doll houses, whatever their point of origin, have been placed in this house. To a large degree, this consists of the ubiquitous stenciled rosewood furniture, and some supplemental pieces from Germany (where this furniture originated) have been included.

Of special interest, in the parlor, is a set of this furniture with gilt stenciling not only upon its wooden frames but also on its glistening crimson upholstery. The latter has a look of leather, but since leather could hardly have survived in such mint condition, this may be oilcloth, or some variation thereof (Plate 186). An unusual extension table in this room bears on its top a remarkable pattern which appears complete whether its two leaves are in or out.

119 The Towgood House (exterior); mid-nineteenth century; 28½" high

A worn and faded page covered with an antique script heightens the charm of this small, slender, mid-nineteenth-century town house from England. The rare page is an inventory of the original contents—undated and unsigned, but with a clue, invisible till held to the light, a watermark: "Towgood's Extra Super." Edward Towgood & Sons, Ltd., still manufacturing paper, offers us forty-four years, from 1836 to 1880, during which such paper was in use. The style of the house and the penmanship of the inventory place the page and the house in the earlier years of this range.

"Inventory of Lilliput House" is the heading, and the modest contents of three rooms, kitchen, drawing room, and bedroom (one on each of the three floors), are carefully set down. It is interesting to see what were considered the essentials in a well-run baby house at mid-century. We note "bellows" and "toasting fork" in the kitchen and "jug and basin" and "towel rail" in the bedroom, but nothing can be more arresting than the list of occupants themselves, departed at some unspecified date but of unmistakable family to judge from their highly specific names. When the inventory was drawn up, most of them were assembled in the drawing room, a cozy company consisting of "Mr. Woodhead, Miss F. Woodhead, Mr. Firbody, Harry Firbody, and Lucy Woodhead & Doll." "Betty the Cook and Mary the Housemaid," their family tree (fir?) unspecified, were properly below-stairs, while "Mrs. Woodhead & Baby" were in the bedroom. The owner of the small house will never see an unidentified jointed wooden in future without wondering if she or he did not, perchance, once reside in this neat-fronted, red brick house with its lace-edged blinds and metal door knocker.

120 The Towgood House (interior); mid-nineteenth century; 28½″ high

Four pieces of furniture and the kitchen fireplace came along with Towgood House and its inventory at the time of its purchase. The tin kitchen grate with its tin fender obviously is original, having been built into the chimneypiece.

It is difficult to date the other pieces. They are of the soft-lead filigree which a factory in Bavaria has been turning out since 1799, and up to the present! Some of the pieces are still being made from the original molds, a fact which makes dating difficult. But these pieces are unmistakably Victorian. The small cupboard with door below and shelf above has a feature which we have never seen else-where—a molded-in lead lamp base with glass chimney and bristol shade. The washstand with its basin opening features not only a built-in mirror but also a red-painted lead candle in a candleholder at either side of it. On the chest, the mirror swivels, and the three drawers work; on the dresser, the door above is missing, but the doors below are in working order. All of these pieces are of the usual silver lead with the gilt wash often found on earlier pieces for embellishment.

One of the charms of this house is its diminutive size. It lends itself to furnishings of perhaps three-fourth-inch scale (¾″ to 1′) and, since doll house furniture of the early-Victorian period seems most often to come in one-inch scale or larger, it is something of a challenge to complete the furnish-ing of such a house. Among the rosewood pieces with gilt stenciling are a square piano (all of 5″ long), a dresser with shelves above and doors below, a marble-topped dressing table, a méridienne—the Mme. Récamier type of sofa with open end—complete in purple silk with roll cushion, and a half-tester bed, its vestiges of gossamer violet curtains clinging to their lace edgings (Plate 169).

121 The South Jersey (interior); mid-nineteenth century; 44″ high

Inside the South Jersey, even though floors were warped and uncarpeted and no shred of drapery remained when the house was found, much evidence lingered of the children (as well as the mice) whose house it had been. A few of the ten, small, paneled, hand-carved doors were missing and had to be replaced. Scrap pictures had been stuck on the ceilings, covering parts of the original, charming, hand-painted designs. Smudge marks on walls and ceilings suggested that the small owners had actually lighted long-departed sconces and chandeliers.

A well-built staircase with landing (balustrade unfortunately missing) and two small built-in fireplaces were the only other surviving interior features. Access to the eight rooms, four large and four small, including hallways, is through three hinged doors at the back. The front hall, too small to be readily entered through its rear (kitchen) door by a full-sized hand, lends easier admittance through the double front doors. The large rooms, fifteen by twenty-four inches, offer the same imposing impression as many of the sizeable, high-ceilinged chambers of their day. A large garret, another typical feature, is formed by the mansard roof. The present owner, early in her collecting days, took the liberty of adding a bathroom to the rear upstairs hall where probably none existed before. Such a rash addition she might, in her maturity, have resisted.

The furnishings, which have of course been collected, include many choice pieces illustrated in particularized plates to follow. A detail picture of the small kitchen is shown. Shelves above the stove were made from pieces of vintage wood taken from a simple chair.

Color Plate 7: The South Jersey (exterior); mid-nineteenth century; 44″ high

We have written at length of this mid-nineteenth-century house elsewhere (*A History of Dolls' Houses*.) It remains one of the most elaborate American doll houses to be seen anywhere and has even been the setting of a mystery for children (*The Doll House Mystery*, Flora Gill Jacobs, Coward McCann, New York, 1958).

This house was found in 1945 in an antique dealer's barn at Malaga, New Jersey, where it had been steadily deteriorating for about eight years, and has since been restored. It is, as its portrait shows, a stately town house spangled with windows of every description—bay, casement, sash, and dormer. With its dark red and green sandstone façade (made, possibly, by dripping sand on a surface of wet glue), its deep red and blue stained-glass surrounding paneled double doors, and its floral medallions painted upon the convex mansard roof, it is the very essence of a mid-nineteenth-century residence, a rejuvenated and diminutive version of such faded relics, now usually on the wrong side of the tracks, as are seen from train windows on the Eastern seaboard.

Except for one side piece, which guided the restoration, the base of the house was missing, and so was the bit of roof above the mansard. (One likes to imagine that a central turret was also a feature of the original).

French street lamps (marked "DÉPOSÉ JS PARIS") with workable wicks have been mounted at either side of the restored entrance stairs. Since the house opens in back, with two hinged side sections and a lift-out center section, it has been mounted for convenience on a revolving table. Iron reindeer, per tradition, guard its front lawn which is further protected by an old green iron Christmas-tree fence.

122 The Tiffany House (exterior); mid-nineteenth century; 54″ high

It is believed that this stately town house was made for a member of New York's Tiffany family. Clearly a New York town house, its "vaguely Italian detail" is a by-product of what Mr. John Maass (*The Gingerbread Age*, Rinehart, New York, 1957) calls the "Italianate interlude." Here we are given a lovely taffy color rather than the traditional brownstone, but the tall windows and high ceilings of the "company rooms" are plainly evident and the roof cornice is certainly all it should be.

As a doll house, this has a practical feature hitherto unnoticed elsewhere—a staircase in front in strange scale to the house itself but perfectly proportioned for seating its young owner on one side and a companion on the other. Two-thirds of the hinged façade swing open to the left, the remaining third to the right. Double windows on both sides of each story make the window total impressive and the curtain problem formidable.

Color Plate 8: The Tiffany House (interior); mid-nineteenth century; 54″ high

Though its key is missing, the lock on the front of the Tiffany house remains, suggesting that the original owners held the furnishings within in some esteem.

Five pieces which came with the house are believed to be original. These, which are of the dark, polished Biedermeier type, include a fine tester bed, with its original pink silk bed curtains intact, and a marble-topped dresser with the gilt decorations so often imprinted upon pieces of this type traced on the mirror frame, doors and drawer. The original gossamer green silk has deteriorated with age both on the sofa and on the commode, where, used as a curtain, it was meant to conceal the article of convenience within.

The drop-front secretary, such as may be found in several sizes and with varying details in doll houses of the period, has a narrow drawer above and three deep drawers below its writing compartment. Since the lowest of these has no embossed pewter knob as its fellows do, it seems likely that this is intended as a secret drawer. Three small drawers at either side of a small mirror occupy the writing compartment. (Color Plate 11.)

The fireplaces in the drawing-room and upper rooms are built-in originals.

123 Somerville House; mid-nineteenth century; 5′ high

This imposing town house, said to be a copy of an existing house in Somerville, Massachusetts, came to the writer with some of its original furnishings. It bears an astonishing resemblance to the Tiffany House (Plate 122). In addition to the same arrangement of rooms, both have double chimneys, a dentelated cornice under the eaves, and a similar arrangement of windows. (It's almost as though a cousin in Massachusetts had sent a sketch to a cousin in New York!) Even the buff paint with brown trim is very nearly the same.

The Somerville House has the additional distinction of double fireplaces in the drawing room, along with an explicit detailing of paneled front doors and of windows with wooden mullions and transoms. In the Tiffany, the latter are painted on the glass, and the door is a painted sham. At the base of the exterior, instead of the wide stairs thoughtfully provided for the young owner to sit on in the Tiffany, two storage drawers flank a flight of stairs useful only to dolls.

Although most of the surviving furniture is either later than the house or damaged, one interesting piece is an unpainted card table with its original label, that of Samuel Hersey, Hersey Street, Hingham, Mass. According to the McClintocks (Marshall and Inez McClintock, *Toys in America*, Public Affairs Press, Washington, D. C., 1961), who have an excellent list of American toy manufactories in their book, Samuel Hersey made wooden toys ca. 1855–80's. The wood of this table is beautifully smooth, even on the concave side pieces below its hinged top, and it is regrettable that half of this top is missing because the remaining half still swivels perfectly.

124 Pennsylvania Cupboard House; *ca.* 1870; 50″ high

Owing to the sad economic fact that dealers can profit more by selling off the contents piecemeal, it has become increasingly difficult to find an old doll house with its original furnishings. Much household history has been dispersed along with these miniature lares and penates, and collectors and historians must bow to the inexorable laws of (very) small business.

The Cupboard House, found in Pennsylvania in 1945, escaped. Its furnishings, an assortment in several scales, were jumbled in boxes when found, but they make a splendid miscellany to represent a Victorian household quite thoroughly.

With a deferential bow to the elaborate cabinet houses of the Netherlands in the seventeenth and eithteenth centuries, this rather austere cupboard was probably run up by the local carpenter. Other than a pitched roof and a doorbell, the façade, to distinguish it, has only four square doors, one to each room, but the rooms are of noble, high-ceilinged proportions with correspondingly tall windows and the original draperies, cornices, and wallpapers.

There were many treasures among the furnishings, especially a gilded lead chandelier with white bristol globes and workable wicks. Of particular interest is the black and gold japanned tin bedroom suite with a hinged lift-top table (a supply of linen inside), a dresser with looking-glass (vintage undergarments in the drawers), and a tester bed resembling one shown in an early Hull & Stafford (Clinton, Conn.) catalogue. The table appears to be identical to one pictured by a Philadelphia tin toy manufactory, Francis, Field & Francis, and since the Cupboard House and its contents were found near Philadelphia, perhaps this is the most likely source. Some of the bits of linen are marked "Bethel," which Welsh name may be a clue to the lost identity of the long-ago owner.

The beguiling parlor mantelpiece provides a specific footnote about a type of needlework popular in the seventies. The fringed lambrequin on the mantelshelf, with edgings to match on the what-not shelves below, is covered with the pillow lace known as macrame. This knotting of fine ecru twine was, according to Frances Lichten, "an occupation to which the artistic devoted themselves," even though it was "hard on delicate hands."

125 Eastern Shore Cottage; Victorian; 22″ high

Another bit of regional architecture, this pleasing cottage from Maryland's Eastern Shore is an accurate reflection of many a small house of Victorian vintage (minus Victorian characteristics) to be seen in that picturesque region.

A careful carpenter—perhaps a father or brother—made this small building with its two rooms, one upstairs and one down, and its open back. The walls are unfinished, but there is a piece of floral carpet on the lower floor and curtains at the numerous glass windows. The exterior is attractively painted a dull green with grey trim.

126 Beverly House; Victorian; 39″ high

Although this unusual house from Beverly, Massachusetts is not large, its slender façade, erect and prim as an ancestor in a New England portrait, stands tall. There is evidence that a chimney once crowned this pleasing exterior, making it taller still.

A dozen glass windows, six to a side, light the rooms within, but the front surprises with matching panes painted on the wood, under cornices identical to those above the glass windows. The double front doors are also hand-painted rather than actual, but all the painting is done with style and charm, including delightful freehand decorations inside the hinged house front.

Always an intriguing starting point for research, an address, "46 Hunt," is painted on the doors. Obviously this small house and its contents were prized, since a key now missing once turned a lock next to the second-story windows. Unfortunately, except for the white dotted swiss curtains, a few pictures, and one charming "ogee" mirror with gilt liner, the once treasured contents have been dispersed, but the three rooms, one to a floor, have their original papers and preserve the flavor of what remains an unusual and appealing doll residence.

127 Massachusetts Victorian; 46″ high

It is intriguing to discover that there is not only regional architecture but, occasionally, a kind of regional *doll house* architecture. A certain type of Victorian doll house from Massachusetts which bears such a regional trademark tends to feature dark-stained wood in both the interior and exterior, an open front, an attic room or two, and a widow's walk at the top.

The house shown opposite follows such a pattern with the exception of the walls, papered in lush Victorian patterns, but undoubtedly added later in the history of the house which originally was unpainted. The restoration, unfortunately anonymous, is almost as interesting as the house itself, imposing a vivid Gay 'Nineties decor upon an earlier, more somber interior. (Although the author's preference is always to leave these treasures from the past as they were, none of *these* alterations is disfiguring or even irremovable.) There are exquisite curtains and draperies in each of the four principal rooms (the kitchen has been unceremoniously abolished) and colorful, intricately beaded chandeliers.

The nice staircase features carved newel posts which match the posts on the widow's walk, and the attic room has a fitted section with a stained-glass window which lifts out. The front, incidentally, has been fitted by its owner with sliding glass panels, a simple and useful means of preserving the contents of open-front houses from dust, children, and inquisitive family cats.

128 Victorian Seaside Cottage; 22″ high

Certain doll houses, like certain houses, have a way of evoking identical responses in a variety of people. This Victorian cottage with its porches at front and side was found in Pennsylvania which, of course, has no coastline, but many a viewer upon seeing it has exclaimed, "It's a seaside cottage!" (Possibly it originated in neighboring New Jersey). Curiously enough, the present owner first saw this doll house in another state, on a table facing the bay in Annapolis, and for her, the array of windows, the first-and second-story ones unusual with frosted patterns and the mansard ones bright with green glass, will always be shimmering with water.

A sure and patient hand fashioned the shingled roof, the ornate bays, the dentelated moldings, and the pierced tin shutters which may be opened and closed. No detail is omitted, from the blue and white stained-glass front door panel to the rain gutters and downspouts—the only doll house ones we have personally seen. The back of the house opens in two hinged sections, and within, the original old wallpapers survive, though the four-room interior, like the exterior, anticipates renovation. The most delightful detail in the interior is the "wall-to-wall" straw matting which many inhabitants of houses during the late nineteenth century knew as an inevitable feature. The mansard roof is open which causes one to wonder wistfully if a section containing a cupola might not be missing.

129 Michigan House (exterior); late Victorian; 60″ high

Sometimes one is suspicious of the perfection of certain doll houses. Were they made as toys or as models? One can have no such doubts about the Michigan House; its architecture is nothing even the most tireless model-maker would wish to commemorate. Its façade begins bravely at the bottom with an elaborate porch across the front, interrupted only by a proper staircase. But the little balcony formed by the top to this porch is pathetic. With the graceless space between its small door and the third story windows, it is like a protruding lip on a homely man which he finds he must camouflage with a moustache. And indeed there has been an attempt at an architectural moustache here—country Tudor paneling has been applied below the windows as a sort of afterthought, as has the tall chimney at the rear of the pitched roof.

Swing open the hinged front and matters are even stranger. A graceful column flanks the door-way on either side of the second-story hall, and an attractive window seat fits into a drawing room bay, not to mention a neat staircase from the second to third floor. But we *must* mention the latter, for how is even the most athletic doll to move between first and second stories? The staircase does not descend to the level of the kitchen and dining room.

In a full-sized house, these matters could be seriously discouraging, but in a doll house even inconveniences are minimized. The Michigan House, with its isinglass windows and dreary original wall-papers but thoroughly furnished in Gay 'Nineties style, is a favorite of doll-house tourists.

130 Michigan House (interior); late Victorian; 60″ high

Furnished in the most ferocious Gay 'Nineties style, inspired by frightening original wallpapers, the Michigan House interior is perhaps the most specific example of a residence which is irresistible in miniature and which would be uninhabitable in full-size.

The crimson paper in the dining room is a case in point. A room 15×16 inches in this paper is warm and vivid; a room 15×16 feet would be impossible—and often was. Wallpaper in Victorian dining rooms, says Osbert Lancaster, was nearly always crimson, a color considered "stimulating to the appetite." Before leaving the smaller room, we point out a remarkable furnishing to be seen at the rear: a red plush sofa built into a superstructure of shelves and mirror, with the resulting nooks and crannies housing an assortment of odds and ends quite capable of intimidating dolls relaxing below, if not of actually crashing down upon them.

In the parlor, on the other hand, the green patterned paper has an elegant sheen, a suitable background for the ormolu furniture. A brass what-not is crowned by a bisque bride and groom under a glass bell, and the parlor table has an album of views of Loch Lomond. (This bride and bridegroom obviously took the Grand Tour rather than the more standard wedding trip to Niagara Falls.) A phonograph with morning-glory horn and a bird in a gilded cage (hanging in the bay window) provide music of divergent styles.

The hall, dividing parlor and study (Plate 162), includes a wall 'phone, a rustic umbrella stand with mirror and shelves above, and a gilded metal, standing card tray—a gilded boy with upraised arms does the standing—complete with cards.

The bedroom at upper right has the standard massive marble-topped pieces, plus that most massive furnishing of all, the armoire. This one, with mirrored doors, is obviously a necessity in a closetless house such as this. The traditional grass mattings, a Victorian necessity for summer floor coverings, may be found on the bedroom floors. This China matting was used all year round by families that could not afford to cover their floors with carpet in winter. The radiators, in a house to which central heating came early, are suitably bronze.

131 Bliss Street; 1895–1910; 27″ high

In the late-nineteenth century, numerous toy manufacturers, both in the United States and abroad, made houses of lithographed paper over wood, but certainly none could have outsold those of R. Bliss of Pawtucket, Rhode Island. Judging by the quantity that have survived, it appears obvious that vast numbers were built, in a variety of styles.

Owing to the fortunate fact that R. Bliss helpfully lithographed his name on every door, and occasionally elsewhere, there is no question about who made his houses. Each of the small buildings on the street above is a Bliss, with the exception of the one (at right) lithographed directly on wood by Converse of Winchenden, Mass. (Plate 133). As arresting an assortment of Gay 'Nineties architecture as one could wish, the houses, fronted with isinglass windows (curtained, when the bits of lace survive), are plentifully supplied with additional lithographed curtained windows on the sides and with gables, dormers, turned wood pillars, and a variety of porches and balconies—the essence of the Queen Anne style which began to succeed Gothic in the 1870's.

Bliss began making these houses in 1895. The largest in the group pictured contains four rooms and a staircase, and the next in size has a single room above and two below. Along with the front, the side of the latter house swings open, giving access to the extra room. All of the houses are wallpapered, both walls and floors.

132 North Carolina Fretwork; *ca.* 1880; 26″ high

This small house owes much of its character to the fret saw, a tool which had a busy revival beginning in the 1870's. Here cornice, balcony, dormers, and widow's walk owe their lacy being to this clever implement.

The house itself is somewhat disappointingly a shell, but such a pretty one, and so very Victorian. Crimson bows tie back net curtains at all the windows, set off prettily from without by the yellow house with its blue-gray trim. There is frosted glass in the paneled front door and red stained-glass above the second floor's double doors. Such a house is always suspect—was it indeed a doll house, or was it in some Victorian realtor's window as a display? Whatever purpose this small building served, it is charming, especially when lighted and furnished to provide alluring glimpses through the windows and its balcony occupied by a nicely dressed bisque lady.

It was found in North Carolina and may very well be a copy of one of the Victorian houses to be seen in Wilmington.

Part II: The Doll Houses & Shops **129**

133 Converse House; *ca.* 1909; 23″ high

A maker of wooden boxes, who accidentally discovered the toy business when he made his small daughter a tea table from a collar box (*Toys in America*), turned Winchendon, Massachusetts into "the Nuremberg of America." His name was Morton E. Converse, and his firm, no longer in existence, was at one time "the largest toy-manufacturing firm in the world."

Among many other toys, he made doll house furniture and houses, and he is represented here by the modest house below. This small house has, lithographed directly on wood, the windows, shingles, and bricks that Bliss and other makers lithographed first on paper. The lithography is necessarily cruder and less detailed, but there are no delicate bits of paper falling off to madden collectors fifty years later. The Converse name is imprinted on the floors inside and on the rugs. The windows are made complete with shades and wallpaper. On the exterior, red shingles and bricks are lithographed, along with a cat in the attic window and even a pair—one to be seen from a window on each side— of identical, rather glum matrons.

134 McLoughlin's Folding House; 1894; 13″ high

Patented in January, 1894 by a Baltimore woman and lithographed in lush Victorian colors by McLoughlin Brothers, this charming arrangement of hinged cardboard makes a successful doll house as well as an attractive collector's item.

As McLoughlin's catalogue pointed out, "It is designed to be played with on a table. A number of little girls may thus get round it to the very best advantage." Parlor, dining room, bedroom, and kitchen are lithographed with every late-Victorian appurtenance or decoration known to wall or floor. Oriental rugs, floral wallpapers, stained glass, plush portieres, an antlered deer head, mantels crowded with bric-a-brac, and even a feather duster are printed upon the premises in the most earnest 1894 fashion. "It is designed to be furnished with paper or other small furniture," the catalogue further noted, "and to be occupied by paper or other small dolls." The "stout binder's board" lends itself to the sturdiest marble-topped pieces, and no proper doll house collection should be without one of these ingratiating toys.

135 Pair of Rooms from Austria; late Victorian; 15″ high

The folding room, frequently French and customarily seen in single form, is here represented in a charming two-room suite. Found in Vienna, this prettily lithographed apartment, the walls of one room besprinkled with lilies of the valley and the other with parrots and pansies, has crimson silk draperies crowned by gilt fringe cornices at its glass windows.

Considerably more sedate than its setting, the fret-work furniture was with the rooms when found. These pieces, meticulously dove-tailed and much more delicately wrought than the fret-work-revival pieces made in such multitudes in the United States in the 'eighties (Plate 167), are wildly divergent in scale (note the chairs in relation to the cupboard in the left-hand room). And there is a curiosity in the form of a wooden sewing machine with workable treadle. Four wooden pegs may be found in one of the twin cupboards, and a shelf in the other. A lovely surprise is that the pegs hold small hats, and the shelf, as are the shelves of all the cabinets, is laden with piles of tiny linens tied in the crispest of narrow blue ribbons. Most of the linen is embroidered and initialed with an infinitesimal "E."

Two brass-framed mirrors, visible between the windows, and two similar, smaller frames to which pictures have been obviously added, are fastened quite firmly to the walls. A blue silk bedspread and pillow with lace appliqué and a dressing table draped in matching materials (with matching pin cushion!) were also with the rooms when found—all in pristine condition.

In the detail picture below, a very similar folding two rooms may be seen, also, interestingly enough, from Vienna. Somewhat smaller, this one is considerably less elaborate. There are lace curtains, but not in combination with red silk draperies as in the other, and they have gilt paper trim rather than gilt fringe. The lithography is also less lush, and one suspects these two rooms and the furniture which accompanied them of a somewhat later origin. The nice family of doll house dolls, circa 1890, came from Vienna with the rooms.

136 A "Mighty Oak" Pair; late Victorian; 12½" high, 47½" wide

Unlike the pairs of lithographed cardboard rooms from Vienna, this sturdy wooden pair does not fold into a box. Indeed, with these sizeable proportions and stout construction, the attacks of the most destructive small brother might have been ineffectual.

The style of the pilasters and other structural details are very like those of the German stores and kitchens of similar vintage, and it seems likely that this "house" was turned out by one of the same makers. The oak wainscoting, with numerous applied wooden embellishments (the pilasters have appliqués of embossed brass) and the dentelated matching cornice are vivid reminders of what Mr. Osbert Lancaster (*Here, of All Places*) calls "Wimbledon Transitional," a turn-of-the-century predecessor of his "Stockbroker's Tudor."

Perhaps the most intriguing feature is the window alcove with two steps and a railing. Under a layer of wallpaper which it was possible to remove without unduly damaging the original paper beneath, a scrap of narrow border paper and the outlines of the rest, framing the walls, was discovered, and one hopes to find a suitable replacement.

The furniture that came with this room is not particularly distinguished (although the tapestry at the left-hand wall of the parlor was someone's absolute inspiration). Some of it has been retained, notably the green plush parlor furniture with center table, and other pieces have been added. There are workable glass casement windows in the bedrooms as well as in the parlor. Because the brass cornice and rod—the only manufactured one, incidentally, we have ever seen, fitted perfectly and irresistibly, it has been hung at the bedroom windows.

137 Leeds Toy House; *ca.* 1903; 22″ high

Perhaps there were instructions printed upon the missing box lid, but without them, an owner devoid of engineering talent required only two or three hours to put this house together, emerging with a most triumphal feeling. Luckily the bottom of the box—the foundation of the house—survived, and on it is printed what one longs to know of all doll houses: "Leeds Toy House. Manufactured by Grimm & Leeds Co., Camden, N. J. Pat. Sept. 22 1903." And then, a final bit of information: "Four Varieties."

   A clever arrangement of folding cardboard with only the porch and roofings reinforced by blocks, the construction is accomplished entirely without glue. Junctions are formed by heavy cardboard pockets in walls which receive cardboard inserts from floors and roofings. This "variety" has four rooms, two up and two down, a dainty sprigged wallpaper, and dark blue window shades behind its isinglass windows. Only one floor strip was sheared off in assembling (the only other damage being the deterioration of strips around the eaves)—a tribute to the strength of the cardboard, after more than sixty years of storage.

138 Gertrude's House; 1904; 34" high

When this house was ordered from Maine on the basis of a brief description, the purchaser was told that a house number was on the door. Such cryptography is always alluring (one dreams of discovering the street name and locating the full-sized original), but in this case the description was inferior to the actuality. A tiny silver plaque is placed on each of the double doors. One of these says "Gertrude," and one says "1904." Who was the fortunate Miss Gertrude, and did she receive her charming toy for Christmas or her birthday? Whatever the details, her house has more than one appealing feature.

The cupola, lighted with three different shades of stained glass, is attached to a removeable roof above the mansard attic. The front façade lifts out readily, the back is open, and a neat staircase with balustrade climbs logically to the attic. The resulting hallways are back to back, with kitchen below and bath above, the latter with a built-in tub and commode and a wonderful bit of oiled paper at the window in a geometric pattern of yellow, red, and black. There are front and back rooms upstairs and down, an open side porch the length of the house, and several sets of handmade furniture obviously made by the same clever carpenter who built Gertrude's house. The furniture includes a handsome parlor set upholstered in crimson and blue velvet and a hall tree with three infinitesimal hooks—all, helpfully, very 1904.

One might have thought the architecture earlier. There is the possibility that the doll house, though built in 1904, was copied from Gertrude's own house of an earlier vintage. There are many pitfalls in dating doll houses.

139 Made in Germany; *ca.* **1900; 32″ high (including chimney)**

One of the real puzzlers to collectors is pinning down the country of origin for many toys, including dolls and doll houses. Even when that welcome fragment, an original shop label survives, the source of manufacture is often still in doubt. A manufacturer's label is even less common, and the difficulties of identification are further compounded by the making of similar wares on both sides of the ocean.

The house pictured is, like many made by Bliss and other factories in the United States, of lithographed paper over wood and of gingerbread architecture. But the unmistakable clue, stamped on the bottom, is in two words: "Gesetzlich geschütz!" Even to those of us who are obliged to consult a dictionary to discover that this is a patent warning, the German source is unmistakable.

It is interesting to note that this house is not only similar in construction but also identical in plan to the largest Bliss house in the author's collection (Plate 131). There is the same arrangement of four rooms, opening in pairs on either side of a staircase. This house is considerably larger, has glass windows rather than isinglass, and varies in architectural detail, but the similarities are striking. Legally registered though it was, the style of this house seemingly inspired others.

140 House with Elevator; *ca.* **1900; 22″ high**

In this small German house, probably from the same maker as the larger specimen in Plate 139, there is the identical front door and knob, brick paper, and other details, plus several additional rather charming embellishments. The window box of flowers on the third floor is a minor one compared to the elevator which substitutes for stairs in the first-and second-story halls. With an inviting upholstered built-in bench, this convenience is operated by a small handle at the base of the house. Attractive doll-house-scale wallpaper lines each of the rooms, and pretty lace-edged curtains may be seen at the windows.

141 Piano-Hinge House; *ca.* 1910; 24″ high

For all its bays and columns, this appealing small house has always seemed of ca. 1910 vintage, the great clue being the bungalow-style dormer modestly crowning the elegance below. This dormer and the front which swings open spang through the middle are operated by piano hinges.

Inside, there are several small surprises. One, having to do with windows, might be useful to a doll house architect. Each glass easily slides in or out of a wooden frame for easy cleaning or repairs. Another trick, perhaps more appropriate to 1910, features a narrow brass rod crossing the ceiling of one of the bedrooms with tiny rings for hanging portieres and, in this case, for dividing one room into two. There is a wide center hall with a tall black-painted mantelpiece with curio shelf above, a simple hat rack, and a staircase with charmingly-turned newel posts. Carved interior columns, window seats, and a mirrored wall in the drawing room are other elegant features.

142 Pennsylvania House; 1912–14; 24″ high

Made by a railroad worker in Pennsylvania over a period of two years, this neat cottage, with minor variations, is likely to bring nostalgia to residents of a number of Eastern states or, at the very least, to make them feel at home. The two years in which it was built were parts of 1912–14, but architecturally it represents an almost indefinable era.

Its clapboard and shingle meticulously applied, the house is engaging with its white and dark green trim and a rusty red roof. An interesting kitty-corner back door, not visible in the picture, and a lift-off panel with lock in back give access to the rooms which downstairs are divided by archways rather than doors. Well-varnished columns flanking the equally well-varnished staircase with its neat balusters and expertly-turned newel posts offer an especially poignant glimpse through the front door.

The same patient and skillful hand fashioned the furniture, as redolent of its era, it will be noted, as the architecture. A few representative pieces are shown, but there is another dark-varnished bedroom "suite," a "brass" bed fashioned somewhat surprisingly of copper tubing, and a dining room set with the inevitable round table and mirrored sideboard. The morris chair has, of course, an adjustable back.

143 Schoenhut Bungalow; 1917; 20½″ high

A Schoenhut catalogue for 1917 describes "a whole new line of doll houses" which the firm had just added, and the bungalow pictured is unmistakably one of these. The well-known Philadelphia firm, famous for its toy pianos, dolls, and circuses, had been founded in 1872 by Albert Schoenhut who had come from Germany after the Civil War. The 1917 catalogue promised that these doll houses would be "less expensive than the fine imported doll houses, but at the same time much stronger, more durable and beautiful."

Judging by the excellent condition of the example pictured, this promise of durability was kept. The small bungalow also has considerable charm. The stairs have nicely-turned balusters and a proper landing; net curtains are on the glass-fronted door and the windows are lace-trimmed; the lithographed wallpapers are exuberant—very striped, very floral, and thoroughly bordered. Perhaps the most amusing feature is one specifically mentioned by the catalogue: lithographed doorways on the walls "showing a perspective view of another room...producing the illusion of a house full of fine rooms." There is a glimpse of a bath with footed tub and a butler's pantry with brightly-patterned oiled paper on the glass doors. There's also a lithographed fire in a lithographed fireplace and lithographed portieres.

On the model pictured, the sides swing open to reveal two rooms apiece, and the roof may be tilted, rather like the lid of an old phonograph, to disclose the top of the staircase and the short walls (this is indeed a bungalow) of two attic rooms.

Schoenhut's DOLL HOUSES
A Line of Very Artistic, High-Class Doll Houses and Bungalows
NEW STYLES AND MODERN ARCHITECTURE

Made of wood and Fibre board embossed to represent stone wall, and roof to represent tile. Inside of houses covered with lithographs to represent fancy wall paper and outside nicely painted in appropriate colors.

Our line of Doll Houses, etc., are made partly out of wood and partly strong, heavy fibre board and will not warp or crack. They are made to open on the side so the children can easily get at all the rooms. The front of the house remains stationary and, therefore, the appearance of the house is not lost by opening.

The foundations of the houses are embossed to resemble genuine rough stone. The outside walls of the houses are embossed and painted to resemble cut-stone and the roofs are made to resemble real tile. Altogether the houses are painted in colors, a fac-simile of the real thing. On the inside the rooms are papered in most modern style of paperhanging. We went to a great deal of expense to have lithographs produced that would give a fine and modern inside finish. In doing this we have adopted a unique idea in not having doorways cut in the partitions from one room to the other, but have the doorways lithographed on the wall showing a perspective view of another room inside of the doorway frame, producing the illusion of a house full of fine rooms.

BUNGALOW, TWO ROOMS
Sizes, 19¾ in. x 20½ in. x 16½ in.

II The Rooms

144 1920's House: Tootsietoy; chair 1⁵/₈″ high

It is always with reluctance that one must confess that the years of one's childhood—in this case the 1920's—have become an era. But the 'twenties have indeed taken a shape, distinct and plain, for all to perceive. Here, we have elected to show just two examples, a nursery (Plate 145) and a set of "living room" furniture, a term which perhaps at this point replaced "parlor" and "drawing room." This set is filled mostly with pieces from the atelier of Tootsietoy, a Chicago factory of frightening name which crowded the doll houses of the 'twenties as full of metal as the ones of the 'fifties were crammed with plastic. The over-stuffed living room "suite," probably meant to represent velour, is as realistic as brightly-painted orange and green metal can make it (surprisingly and terribly realistic indeed), and such accessories as floor lamps and hand-wind phonographs heighten the illusion.

Actually, Tootsietoy was at its best in kitchen and bathroom furnishings, all of which look literally at home in metal, especially in white but obtainable in numerous colors. In 1928, the firm advertised bathrooms "in the new orchid and green finishes" and kitchens in "two new colors, red and green, just like the colorful kitchens so in vogue." The other rooms were also available in a range of colors, epitomizing the rainbow-colored angularity of a mode which swept away the era of dark and varnished curves that preceded it.

As described in toy catalogues of the 'twenties and early 'thirties, the line offers enough information about the period to furnish a standard essay upon its furnishing and decorating. There is even, along with the French grays and Chinese reds, a comment upon architecture. In 1930, the firm presented the "Tootsietoy Mansion . . . designed by one of America's greatest architects who specializes in the Spanish type of architecture." In short, the rise of Hollywood, which drew more general attention to the West in all its aspects including its buildings, left its mark even on miniature houses.

145 1920's House: The Nursery; 10¼″ high

To show that doll houses were not entirely dependent upon painted metal (Plate 144) in the 'twenties, we offer the nursery with wooden furniture from New England, neatly made and nicely painted (pink), and an assortment of well-made supplementary pieces both imported and domestic.

The identical four-poster bed, two-drawer dresser, and wood-bottom rocker are shown in F. A. O. Schwarz' 1923 catalogue. With an arm chair, it was available in pink and pale blue at $8.50. It was, according to the catalogue, "made in New England by an experienced artisan." This was Tynietoy whose small catalogue we recently examined through the courtesy of Mrs. Preston Weatherred, Jr. of Houston, Texas. Advertising their wares as "Correct Miniature Reproductions of Antiques," M. I. Perkins and A. Vernon of Providence, Rhode Island offered both houses and furnishings. A handsome colonial mansion, unfurnished with garden, cost, even in those days, $170. Without garden, it was $145; furnished, with garden, $247. Furnishings were reasonably priced.

The 1920's House itself, which has only a pitched roof, a cumbersome staircase, and some rather needless windows and interior doors, is nevertheless of a type well-suited to such display. Old glass-fronted bookcases, papered, carpeted, and lighted as this has been, make excellent doll houses, especially when they have adjustable "ceilings" for rooms of all periods. (After papering and carpeting all the rooms in this house, the author recommends the process only to the patient.)

146 Pennsylvania Cupboard House Parlor; *ca.* 1870; 18″ high, 18″ wide

As a representative parlor, the high-ceilinged chamber in the Pennsylvania Cupboard House has such advantages as its original wallpaper, curtains, and gilt cardboard cornices. Another interesting accessory, perhaps by the same hand which fashioned the curtains, is the fringed lambrequin on a black and gilt wooden mantelpiece with fringed shelves for bibelots. The tall cupboard with bone ornamentation came with the house and so did the étagère, a piece laden with such treasure as a miniscule bisque trinket box in which Jenny Lind's skirt forms the base and the rest of Jenny and her little dog form the lid. Both the workable table lamp and the crystal chandelier which, augmented by a tiny electric bulb, casts lovely shadows upon the ceiling, were additions from France.

Although all of the bric-a-brac which was found with this house is wonderfully representative, with even a conch shell (a miniature version thereof) to put at the base of the mantelpiece and a repoussé brass vase to hold tinted grasses, two additions could not be resisted: a deck of mid-nineteenth-century playing cards laid for solitaire on the inevitable center table and the family album, its metal clasp open, with a flower marking the photograph of a contemporary figure who seems an appropriate member of any miniature family, General Tom Thumb.

147 French Folding Parlor; *ca.* 1880; 9″ high, 16″ wide

France has made a charming specialty of the single miniature room which often folds into a box. All in green and gold, with its green draperies edged in gilt paper and its lace undercurtains intact, this small parlor is an ingratiating example.

Along with the walls (tiny gilt stars on green paper) and the glass windows, two small gilt-paper-framed pictures and a pair of sizeable gilt-paper-framed mirrors fold into the box. The latter has a green-patterned base which forms the floor of the room.

Delicately scroll-cut of light wood with a fine strip of paper applied to resemble inlay, the furniture includes an oval tea table, five chairs with fringed-upholstered seats, a console with two shelves, and an imposing cupboard or dresser with doors below and scroll-cut shelves above. A more curious piece, resembling a fireplace but revealing shelves when its drop front is lowered to the floor, is covered in the same dark green, leather-like material that covers the chair seats. An embossed metal clock with paper face has a gilt shepherdess and sheep above and the same leather-like base below.

A Sevres tea set, a collection of painted miniature French porcelains, and several small books including *Bijou Pictures of Paris* and *Les Rondes de l' Enfance,* the latter with music and illustrations and dated 1895, have been added.

148 Victorian Drawing Room; 8¼″ high, 17″ wide

Although most of the rooms described in nearby pages are French, France did not have a monopoly on the individual room. These papered wooden walls are possibly German, or even American; the presence of the French furniture is arbitrary. The room was purchased with furniture obviously too large for it and plainly not original, and this was replaced.

The drawing room set shown here is of special interest. Almost identical to a set in the South Jersey doll house (Plate 121), this came from New Hampshire in its original paper-covered wooden box. Only fragments of the faded blue-printed paper remain. Inside the hinged lid someone has carefully printed "TOY FURNITURE 100 YEARS OLD—1850," and then hand-written, "in the Graddon family. Please take care of it."

It is interesting to note the few variations between this and the set in the South Jersey House. Here the upholstery is of blue silk, where in the South Jersey it is a charming print of birds and flowers in rust and blue and green. The only two structural differences are in the desk which, otherwise identical, has here a green baize panel on its writing surface and a pull-out leaf in front. Since elaboration usually is to be found in earlier pieces, one suspects that this set is older than the more gaily upholstered version.

The carpet has been mounted on cardboard and laid (by a tackless, glueless method!) over the rather severe, printed "tile" floor. Late for this room, the phonograph with morning-glory horn got in by virtue of charm, a sometimes irresistible attraction.

149 "Very Little, Very Funny" Salon; Victorian; 6³/₈″ high, 11″ wide

Just as a word heard for the first time seems often to turn up again within twenty-four hours, so does this sort of coincidence frequently extend to more tangible matters. Shortly before a photograph of this tiny parlor came in the mail from the French Riviera, the writer, having never seen one like it before, bought an identical room from a Florida dealer. Since the two tables are missing from the latter, the picture shown is of the example belonging to Mme. Madeleine Schlumberger of Biot, A. M., France. It is also irresistible to use Madame's own description (in her charming blend of English and French) of this "very little, very funny... (salon) of unbelievable colours." After describing these colors—the orange floor, the "violent blue" walls, the pale nile green curtains, the violet velvet upholstery, the white, vermillion, dark green, and black furniture of lithographed paper on wood—she comments: "When 'bad taste' reach such an intensity, it seems to me genius! I call this 'salon of a Munich cocotte en retraite!' " This lovely comment is offered without further ado.

It is not within the province of this book to comment on the many remarkable collections which have been learned of within recent years, but a note about Madame Schlumberger's delightful collection cannot be resisted. Although as a rule the writer prefers antique doll rooms as found, Madame, an artist, has created her small world, a representation of her family's history, with a blend of antique doll house pieces and her own handiwork which is both imaginative and beautiful.

150 1892 Dining Room in Paper; size; 15″×16½″

To the doll-house historian, there is something fully satisfying about a sheet of cardboard furniture, absolutely uncut. No out-of-scale hand has ventured to move the be-laced, be-ribboned pin cushion from the dresser; the scalloped fringe on the table lamp shade is in pristine condition; the position of the britannia butter dish, the crumber and tray, and the dresser scarves are exact historical facts, precisely preserved.

When we may add to all this fascinating minor information an exact name and date and place, we feel practically sent back in time, like those characters in historical fantasies who swallow a special potion and are wafted into 1876 or 1892 or some other distant era. In this case, we are wafted to 1892, the specific year in which "Our Dining-Room," "Our Parlor," and "Our Bedroom" (Plate 166) were copyrighted by one F. Cairo of Brooklyn. From the turkey red bed-spread to the bright green dining room settee, it is an informative visit.

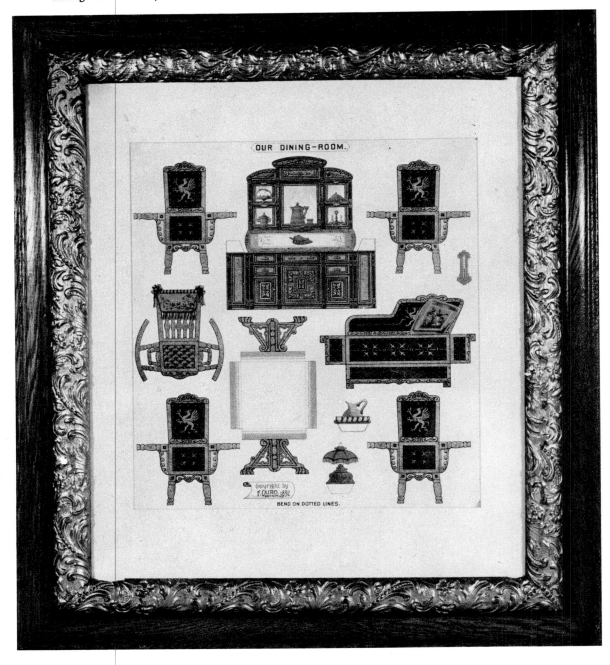

Color Plate 9; A Victorian Dining Room; *ca.* 1880; 13¾" high, 15" wide

"The wall paper was always dark and nine times out of ten of a self-patterned crimson design; that colour being considered, quite rightly, as stimulating to the appetite." So writes Osbert Lancaster of the Victorian dining room. The Victorian doll house dining room was no exception. The one shown (from the Michigan House) is papered in a shade as red as rare beef.

Although the extension table, with its two workable leaves in place, dominates the room, the buffet with its marble surface separating cupboards below from a mirrored superstructure above, is imposing. The table, set with a fringed red and white cloth, is laden with an array of blown stemware, bristol dishes, embossed lead cutlery, and fringed napkins in metal rings.

The galleried butler's tray with its metal fringe and folding stand is decorated with a blue and white Delft-type landscape echoed in a plaque that hangs above it. Upon the tray, a china platter containing a handsome lobster nicely garnished with greens awaits the discriminating diner. It is likely that the crumber and tray will be needed since the loaf of bread is real, having been freshly baked some years ago by noted author-illustrator Tasha Tudor as a present to the owner of the house. Less real, but decidedly realistic, are the chairs with their woven "rush" seats and the brass hanging lamp with its Bristol shade.

Since, by virtue of its inedible charm, doll house food is dainty enough to tempt the most jaded appetite, it is a doll house accessory of considerable allure. Mrs. Greene *(English Dolls' Houses)* in her delightful comments upon this delectable subject, uses the word "seductive," and it is logical and appropriate. She reproduces a German catalogue page (Biberach, 1836) illustrating, in lavish assortments, plates and platters of meats and fruits and puddings, alongside the oval pine boxes which contained them.

One of the oldest pieces in our illustration, probably mid-nineteenth century, is the handsome oval tureen of bisque, with a pear for a finial, containing bisque soup or chowder (lobster bisque, perhaps?)

The fish (lower left) casually straddling a plate was made in the small scale shown (the plate is 1¼″) and in a considerably larger scale (that plate is 2⅞″). A number of sets of this food (twelve different dishes to a box) turned up in mint condition in an old Baltimore toy shop in recent years, with a decorated birthday cake, shown in larger scale due northwest of the fish, among the dozen.

Turkeys and other fowl are perhaps most frequently found; in the author's collection but not shown, there is even a representation of a turkey partially consumed. More unusual is the formidable boar's head, apple in mouth and garnished to a fare-thee-well (center above). This handsome group, on porcelain platters, includes (to the boar's left) a dish of eel and (to its right) an assortment of cheeses as well as the inevitable and picturesque lobster. Like the boar's head, all of these dishes are meticulously, if sometimes mysteriously, garnished.

The filigree lead basket with assorted composition cakes (left) is a more unusual combination of materials.

The egg cup and the egg are shown in two versions: a silvery glass cup with a white glass egg and a wooden egg cup with a rooster painted thereon. One wonders what the wooden egg which is contained in the latter and neatly unscrews may once have held. A baby chick, perhaps, or a motto?

The bottled beverages include the customary fifths (sixtieths?) of Scotch, simply so labeled in gilt on black. Wine bottles in delicate shades of green or amber hold the dregs of still-corked but long-evaporated liquids which bear such labels as "Madeira," "Karlonitzer," and "Xeres." More rare is a dark glass bottle with silver foil top and a decorative label in gilt and colors describing a French sparkling wine. Two full-dressed cherubs with sizeable wings uphold a crown. The vintner's name is less legible than the information that he was given the gold medal by Napoleon in 1810.

Perhaps the cumulative noun we have chosen to encompass the infinite variety of tea and dinner sets to be found in miniature is rather a humdrum choice when the charm and beauty of these small wonders is considered, but it must cover all of the materials, porcelain, papier-mâché, metal, and glass, among others, of which they are made, as well as their assorted purposes.

From an era when the tea cup rather than the cocktail glass was the emblem of hospitality, it is not surprising that tea sets may be found in profusion, in miniature as well as in full-size. On the marble stand, one of the innumerable papier-mâché versions may be seen; less common, just below it, on its own tray, is a beauty marked "Sèvres." Representing the tons of metal tea-sets—pewter, britannia, lead, and tin—which served dolls for decades in larger versions, the embossed example on its own tray (right) is rarer in this tiny scale.

The tea set on its traditional painted metal oval tray (left) is of a delicate glass known as Bristol in England and opaline in France. (The rest of us, presumably, may take our choice.) This lovely ware was made for generations in, obviously, dozens of patterns. The specimen shown here has one of the most traditional designs—a soft, rusty-red rose with green foliage similar to a set in Queen Victoria's doll house. Plates showing miscellaneous patterns may be seen in the foreground. Most often this ware is to be found in pure white, a fact to which one attaches an admonition "Be careful in washing"; some patterns (possibly earlier in vintage) are washable; others, as some of us have learned to our sorrow, disappear with the dust.

The tiny set at center, with matching spoons, came packed in a capsule from France. No padding was necessary; the infinitesimal scale seems resistant to large-scale knocks and bumps.

The dinner set (upper right) is distinguished by the presence of its attractive and informative original box. The charming white china pieces with blue floral pattern found in so many mid-nineteenth-century doll houses are pictured on the lid and every piece shown thereon was found intact inside. The only wording on the box, impressed into the cardboard bottom, refers to the box itself: "Mechanische Cartonage Fabrick. Freidr. Christian Bad Soden A, T Patent No. 339828."

Although the breakfast set (upper left) contains items other than "dishes," we offer it here, and with pardonable pride since it too came with its original box. Inside, there were six each of knives, forks, spoons, egg-cups, plates, rolls, and napkins in rings. Like the rolls, the napkins with their rings are of a painted composition, most realistic. All other items are of metal, including the tin plates which are painted white. On the charmingly lithographed box lid, a small black dog pursues a baker's boy in white cap and apron who is bearing aloft a prettily garnished and towering confection. A castle, very Spanish in appearance, with red tile roof may be seen in the background, and what is most interesting, the label of a Barcelona toy shop is still affixed to the bottom of the box. The price and part of the label have been partially obliterated, but "RAMBLA ESTUDI" may also be discerned.

The identity of the lovely tea service on a silver tray (left-center) was a mystery until just before this volume went to press. Then a re-examination of some Raphael Tuck post cards of the Queen's Dolls' House, the celebrated miniature house presented to Queen Mary in 1924, revealed a set identical in appearance. The official Raphael Tuck card identified it as a set made at Stoke-on-Trent, without naming the factory. A few days after this discovery, a post card from a German friend presented a remarkable—and conflicting—coincidence. From a small museum in Würzburg, Museum Lydia Bayer, a duplicate of this set was pictured and its presentation to the British royal family noted—but its manufacture was attributed to Dresden! Because of the connection between the British and German royal families, it seems altogether likely that a presentation from Dresden would have been made to Queen Mary's Dolls' House. In any case, the mark on the porcelain tray (not pictured) is a Dresden mark, and the Raphael Tuck post card, however official, was evidently in error.

153 Glassware

The term "glassware" is here employed to define those pieces which are traditionally made of glass—stemware, tumblers, decanters, and such. But it seems pertinent to refer, at least, to the lovely tea and dinner sets of Bristol glass (Plate 152) which were made in such numbers for Victorian doll houses.

Sometimes the delicate glass is combined with embossed lead or pewter, as in the green glass beverage set of pitcher and goblets (center), the green glass comport (right), and the three tumblers (left).

Most choice are the wines with air twist stems (center), somewhat larger in scale than the others, of an eighteenth-century style which occurred in many variations. The "twist" at the left is a blue-edged white ribbon of infinite delicacy; with magnification, four white strands may be seen within the blue. The somewhat coarser example at the right consists of four green threads braided into two heavier white cords.

Two interpretations of hobnail in miniature may be seen in the carafe (upper right), and the larger goblet in the group (bottom right). Of similar appealing delicacy are the ribbed pieces with lidded pitchers (lower left) which are believed to be Georgian. We have neglected to show an ingenious set of spun-glass wines in which the red liquid is indicated by the use of red glass and a set of considerably later style in which an actual facsimile, now mostly evaporated, was contained by an infinitesimal cork in the stem.

Perhaps the rarest pieces here are the vase and decanter (bottom center), the only two pieces of miniature cut-crystal we have seen.

154 Early Nuremberg Kitchen (I); *ca.* 1800; 17″ high, 36″ wide

To prove that educational toys are not in the least modern and the meticulous German *hausfrau* not in the least accidental, we submit the Nuremberg kitchen which, agleam with rows of brass pans, pewter plates, and copper pots, has traditionally instructed small German daughters in the household arts.

"Eighteenth century," which we originally applied to the specimen pictured, was unquestionably broad, but kitchens, even more than doll houses, possibly because metal is so much sturdier than wood, tend to become accumulations of objects handed down mixed with later additions. Dating them becomes hazardous, but we venture to say ca. 1800 of this one after studying a picture of a kitchen so dated at Augsburg. Several important utensils are common to both kitchens.

All Nuremberg kitchens have the inevitable hooded oven with a chimney to carry off the smoky fumes. Charcoal used for cooking on the brick hearth was stored in the opening below it—concealed in our photograph by the handsome copper firescreen. The latter was set on the hearth to protect the person revolving the spit from the heat of the fire. This screen is identical to the one pictured in the Augsburg kitchen, and so is the large copper vessel with hinged lid suspended between two metal brackets above the open fire on the hearth. The position of this imposing utensil assured a continuous supply of hot water all day long. The lidded copper jug beneath the scales, used to carry the water, is also identical to one in the Augsburg kitchen, and there are numerous other similarities.

Matching copper pots in graduated sizes, hanging by their own small brass rings, are lined with tin. Such cooking pans were popular for generations, but "in spite of the highly attractive appearance of a polished and gleaming *batterie-de-cuisine* of this metal," say *The Connoisseur Period Guides,* "the 1850's saw the introduction and acceptance of the more hygienic and more easily managed enamelled iron."

In the left foreground, an early, finely hand-crafted pewter porringer may be seen. Also of special interest, on the hearth, is a tin lamp which burned fat in the cup beneath its lid, a wick emerging from its spout and with a saucer base to catch the drippings.

155 Early Nuremberg Kitchen (II); eighteenth century; 16½″ high, 32¾″ wide

One might write a fulsome essay on the variety of objects, dominated by a dazzling array of pewter, to be found in this small, be-shelved rectangle. Heavy brass skillets flank the traditional hooded oven, hanging above skewer racks which once supplied a turnspit. Customary metal rings of lighted charcoal for surface cooking are implied by black painted circles on the oven surface. A harshly realistic accessory is the poultry coop, to the right, where the unfortunate occupants were fattened on kitchen scraps. A copper kettle stands on a tin brazier, here placed on top of the oven. Next to it is a stacked series of pewter hot dish carriers, threaded together with a leather thong of which a counterpart, we are told, is still in use in India. On the wooden trestle table, the oval fish stew pan is one of several handsome pewter pieces with mushroom finials on their lids. A matching low sectional container with sliding top, probably for spices, is on the left-hand counter. Not very visible next to this is an egg cooker, a two-tiered multi-holed rack in which eggs might be uniformly immersed for boiling.

The decorative detail with which many of these small pieces are made is folk art at its most alluring. A delicate leaf pattern which appears to be hand-wrought embellishes a pewter salt box, while nearby, a pair of embossed pewter birds build a pewter nest with pewter twigs on the upper side of a fuel carrier. Minute brass appliqués ornament a set of graduated tin collanders.

156 Nuremberg Kitchen Cook Book; 1858; size: 4″ × 5″

Even if only the cover of this small cookbook with its charming illustration had survived, it might still have been considered a treasure, but it is intact, faded and a bit wrinkled, like an elderly cook, and weathered by the heat of the oven and possibly a little gravy.

Printed in Nuremberg in 1858, the title page informs us in German that this is a "Little Cook Book for the Doll's Kitchen," or "First Instruction for Cooking for Girls 8–14 Years of Age." So worded, this inscription is an explicit corroboration—if more is needed—that such toys were true educational toys, specifically intended for instruction as well as for play.

This small wonder was found with the Nuremberg Kitchen II, a mid-nineteenth century addition to its hoard of pewter and copper of earlier date.

Kochbüchlein

für

DIE PUPPENKÜCHE

NÜRNBERG

Joh: Phil: Raw'sche Buchhandlung

(C. A. Braun.)

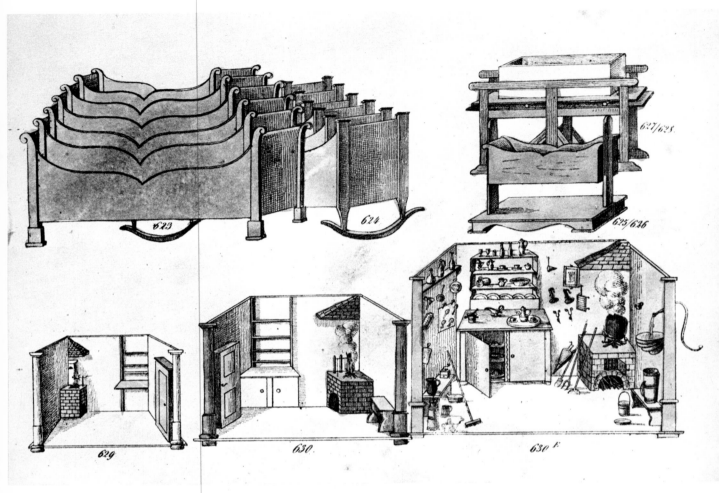

157 Kitchens and Miscellanea in a German Toy Catalogue, *ca.* 1848

KITCHENS

Wooden floor and walls with window. Each contains a stove and set of Kitchen Utensils, also Wooden Furniture. Sizes of one room Kitchens range from 14 inches to 35 inches in width.

Prices according to size.......**$2.00, $2.50, $3.50, $3.75, $4.00, $6.50, $7.50,**
12.75, 15.00

Kitchens with Pantry, 25 inches...........**$4.00**   33 inches. **$8.00**

Color Plate 10: Victorian Kitchen with Pantry; 12″ high, 24½″ wide

The appealing blue Onion Meissen patterned paper above a blue and white "tile" dado is a distinguishing feature of this Victorian kitchen, as is the adjoining pantry. The latter, papered in faded red sprinkled with tiny gilt stars, contains a pair of built-in plate rails, perhaps, along with the three painted fixtures attached to the wall of the kitchen proper, the only original pieces remaining. The fixtures, which include the long shelf supported by porcelain pins and the utensil rack (the wooden-handled porcelain potato masher, skimmer, etc. have been added), are painted ivory like the frame of this beguiling two-room affair.

An interesting kitchen set of dark oak has been introduced, including a table, salt box, dough tray, dish cupboard, pie safe with stiff cloth mesh for ventilation, and an irresistible spice rack with five labeled drawers. The most complex piece is the icebox with fancily embossed hinges, a pierced brass circular vent, wire racks, and a lift top which reveals two bottles of wine on most realistic ice. An incomplete piece, not shown, is a pot-lid rack, which, interestingly enough, is exactly like the ivory one at the upper left which came with the kitchen.

From a different source than the kitchen set, the marble-top dresser in the pantry, its fancy lead hooks at the sides hung with skimmer, cleaver, and other utensils, is the only one of its genre this collector has ever seen.

The detail picture, from a 1913 F.A.O. Schwarz catalogue, shows a kitchen pictured by the firm in catalogues as early as 1894 and as late as 1918. In type, it is not unlike the kitchen pictured in our larger photograph.

158 Late Victorian German Kitchen; *ca.* **1895; 15½″ high, 36″ wide**

The variety of miniature kitchens made during the eighteenth and nineteenth centuries is astonishing, from the early Nuremberg examples with their lovely hand-wrought copper and pewter implements to the ones manufactured in quantity until as late as World War I. That the later ones could be as elaborate as the most choosey small cook could wish is thoroughly demonstrated by this sizeable German specimen with its splendid clutter of furnishings and utensils.

The tin stove which has an alcohol-trough beneath, can actually cook a (very) small dinner. The curious, red-painted "Eismachine" with its white porcelain finial will not only make real ice cream but also has recipes, in French and German, on a page rolled up inside. A printer's symbol for 1894 on this sheet helps to date the whole.

Most of the plenishings came with this kitchen and probably originated with it. Some pieces of enamel-ware of blue, white, and granite have been added to similar pieces, and there have been other additions, such as the tin icebox and the rack for "Sand, Seife, and Soda," a trio meant for scrubbing German tile floors (in this kitchen represented by a lovely stenciled pattern on wood). The chair which converts to a ladder is a combination often also used for library steps. A tin rack with hooks on which to hang towels for glassware, silver, and china, labeled in German, harks back to an era of more meticulous and careful housekeeping than most of us have time for today.

159 Tin Kitchen; late Victorian; 9½″ high, 17½″ wide

A traditional Victorian toy, the tin kitchen, often stenciled or embossed, with a hooded stove in the center and a pump to one side, still survives in some quantities. Although these are oftenest found with the original utensils replaced and in varying stages of peeling paint, bent tin, and general disarray, the small kitchen pictured, which came out of an old store, is believed to be intact, with its original pots, molds, and scoops still hanging on its tiny hooks.

Such kitchens as this were made by the thousands, many of them in the United States, ranging from ones a few inches square with a few utensils to ones perhaps two feet long with such extra fittings as a built-in tin cupboard and a lavabo.

Part II: The Doll Houses & Shops **157**

160 Kitchen Stoves

Those delectable plaster foods to be found in doll kitchens obviously were cooked by honest cooks in honest ovens. From the wood-burning range to the gas stove, there is almost no method of roasting, broiling, or baking undemonstrated in miniature.

Having evolved from the Robinson (1780), Carron, and Bodley (1802) ranges, the English grate with broiler and oven (above left) was a fixture in British Victorian kitchens, replacing the spit and grill (Plate 154) of the eighteenth century. As the *Britannica* points out, "A single century has seen greater improvement in methods of cooking than in all the previous years in which man has had to eat." Coal replaced wood as a fuel, gas replaced coal, and gas now shares the burden with electricity. Daisy, the iron gas range (right), is an early miniature example, but we learn with surprise that gas for cooking was used to a moderate degree in the United States as early as 1859, chiefly with stoves imported from England, and that many types of gas ranges were exhibited at the 1876 Centennial.

The iron open-hearth stove with the fuel door on the side (center), being earlier, is less commonly found in miniature than the ubiquitous wood-burning range of which an example may be seen on each side of the triangular stove in the foreground. The latter, which are currently being reproduced in larger sizes from the old molds, usually have such names as "Baby," "Tot," "Gem," and "Star" molded into their door-fronts. Of more interest is the claw-footed stove (third from right rear) with burnished brass door and three removeable plates with workable wicks below. (From just such a toy stove, though of considerably larger size, a luncheon was once served to the writer!) The triangular tin stove in the foreground is rather rare. The only other corner range we have seen in miniature is in the Early Victorian House (Plate 114). A bottle-jack and screen, which device for roasting was used in combination with the English kitchen fireplace, is shown in Plate 161.

161 Some Kitchen Utensils

Perhaps for the same reason that kitchens themselves have been such popular toys, kitchen accessories are to be found in dazzling variety. One of our favorites, to the left of the plate rack which presides over this group, is the bottle jack and screen, a nineteenth-century rotisserie which stood before the kitchen fireplace. The jack, hung from the top, turned; the meat, suspended from a hook, dripped into a small drip-pan below; and the roasting screen protected the cook from the intense heat when she reached through to baste the meat. (On a full-sized jack of this sort, a clock-type spring was wound by a key.)

Below the rotisserie, a pewter ice-water pitcher with its own cup attached to a built-in hook stands next to a chafing dish which is divided into three sections as the real ones were. This piece is of the same late-Victorian vintage as the swinging tea kettle on stand to its right; judging from the numbers which survive, both toys were made in great quantities.

Below the kettle, and flanked at either side by a fish stew pan and fish trivet, is a fish platter. All three pieces are Georgian, and the fish patterns embossed upon them are exceptionally detailed and beautiful. Also quite irresistible is the graduated set of pewter dish covers (right), the blue ceramic pudding mold (below), and the fruit knives with rack (right). A salt box and a single pudding mold (far left), two pieces molded in lead with a copper wash, represent a whole set of kitchen pieces in this ware—ladles, molds, measures, and such. A mere selection must serve to show the variety in which knife boxes, cutlery, napkin rings, mortars with pestles, and other kitchen appurtenances are to be found.

162 Father's Study: Michigan House; late Victorian; 13½″ high, 12″ wide

For as evocative a room, nostalgically speaking, as one might wish, we offer Father's Study from the Michigan House. Empty when it arrived, this house afforded this room, with wallpaper of a drab brown; and papa, with a large moustache and a purple weskit beneath his suit jacket, moved in.

Presently taking a snooze on his brown leather couch, his pup resting between his ankles, he may be presumed at other times to preside over his oak roll-top desk, his early model typewriter (invisible, on an invisible library table—see Plate 219), his ship model, his loving-cup trophies, his mounted deer head, his cards, and his checker game. Another member of the family may have confiscated space for the tank of goldfish. A gilded, upside-down cupid, atop three pointed electric light bulbs, gazes down upon papa as he dozes.

Color Plate 11: Desks and Their Accessories

Those indefatigable letter writers, the Victorians, having had a need for writing furniture beyond that of the spasmodic correspondents of today, appear to have handed down to us an abundance of desks as well as of letters.

As usual, this circumstance is reflected in miniature as well as in full-size. It is true that we have not been left a large number of miniature letters, but we have inherited a goodly assortment of desks. A few examples are shown in our illustration, and there are others, with a related summary, in the introductory chapter.

Two mid-nineteenth-century drop-front examples, one shown open and one closed, feature interesting variations,though both are of the Biedermeier rosewood genre. The one at center is larger in scale, and, as its bone supports and dentelated cornice suggest, it is probably, with this finer detail, earlier than the other, on which embossed gilt paper trims the black-painted supports. Each of these has its small interior drawers at either side of a scrap of mirror. The rosewood desk between these two, also mid-nineteenth century, has the familiar gilt stenciling, while the tiny lady's desk (below right) is of a more classic styling. The wire gallery at the top is a charming embellishment.

The French Empire parlor desk with ormolu legs and matching filigree shelves is more fully discussed in Plate 148. The oak roll-top, which actually is a bank (a disguise we dislike to confess), is, except for a slot inside, otherwise realistic and a perfect example of the late Victorian type.

The range of desk accessories is wide and delightful, as the random specimens suggest. Among them, the inkstands alone are a rather complete comment on writing tools of the eighteenth and nineteenth centuries. Shown side by side, both in porcelain and in pewter, are early examples with cups for ink and sand. Since according to the *Britannica,* blotting paper was known as early as the fifteenth century, it is curious that the use of sand persisted as late as it did. The embossed pewter specimen (upper desk, left) presided over by a bird about to take flight, is German. On other desks, two inkstands in embossed brass, one with hinged brass cups and one with cups of the most gossamer glass, are eloquently Victorian. A roller blotter of embossed brass matches the latter.

On the relatively modern desk at the right is a hinged well with a recess for a pen, along with the pen itself and a roller blotter of green-painted metal. With its sleek styling, this desk set, purchased at F. A. O. Schwarz in approximately 1927, is as distinctly of the 1920's as its neighbors are of their own eras.

Other accessories, such as terrestrial globes (we have never yet heard of a celestial one in miniature), wax jacks, seals, a writing case with letters inside written in very miniature French, and even a "perpetual" calendar, which may be adjusted and used forever, are specific—and irresistible.

163 Books and Magazines

Of all the treasures which may be found in miniature, among the most appealing are the books which, in postage stamp sizes, may be found in sufficient variety to build a sizeable library. Marvels of printing ingenuity, these small volumes are the province of an exclusive group of bibliophiles. Some of the books are exceedingly rare and dear, but many have found their way into doll houses, and no miniature parlor of any pretensions is complete without a few of these beguiling volumes. Such books only incidentally have appeared on doll shelves, but the *English Bijou Almanacs* (the 1836 one pictured has engravings of Byron and Schiller, among others), the French fables, and the late-Victorian Bibles and dictionaries are not the whole story.

Tales are told of full-sized libraries whose uncaring, unreading owners buy books by the yard that have not a single word behind their handsome leather façades, so it is not astonishing that miniature libraries are at times reduced to this printless state. The unusual Biedermeier bookcase pictured features books by the inch—of probable mid-nineteenth century origin to judge by the authors represented. In the small "rosewood" bookcase, decorated in fanciful gilt motifs, lined with traditional blue, and surmounted by an owl in relief, such giants as Voltaire and Goethe keep company with such relatively forgotten authors as Berquin and Uhland. Every one from Aristotle to Franklin may be seen through the glass of the slender Gothic doors with their ivory knobs, and a student of the world's literature might write an illuminating essay about this literary company so indelibly assembled within a toy for children.

A most ingenious library of considerably greater literary detail is arranged in a wood and metal two-tiered hanging shelf, quite obviously from France. A dozen paperback volumes in jackets of green and beige are amusingly presented—on their spines, the author's name, then the phrase "OEUVRES COMPLETES" and, below, "PRIX 300!" or whatever the price may be. On the cover of each, all except price is repeated, plus "PARIS. Chez l'Editeur." Each of these is a sort of box and contains the ingenious gimmick of a page which unfolds from within into a biography of each of these authors, all French and so assorted a company as Mme. de Sevigné, Balzac, and Perault. Since the date of Lamartine's death, 1869, is given, we know that the small books can be of no earlier production, but they are unquestionably Victorian, perhaps of the 'seventies.

To read such infinitesimal print, needless to say, one needs a magnifying glass, or spectacles. Both are shown in the foreground. The gold spectacles have no lenses, but they and their early style case, its two sections linked by a chain, are otherwise perfect examples of verisimilitude.

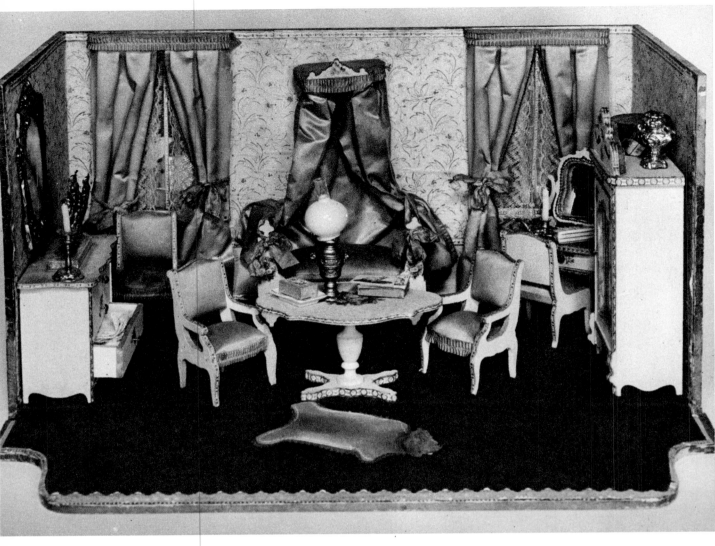

164 French Bedroom; late Victorian; 10″ high, 19½″ wide

Considerably larger in scale and obviously later in vintage than the small boudoir in Plate 165, this French bedroom is elegant in blue satin, with blue wallpaper and the customary pretty floral scrap pictures applied to the table top, cupboard, dresser, and dressing table. One may compare the carpeted floor of crimson fabric with the papered floor in the earlier room. The furniture style, of course, is identical.

A few accessories have been added, notably the curious "bear" rug (in this case a dog!), a soap dish with a blue-wrapped cake bearing New Year wishes, a gilded-lead chamber stick, an ivory clothes brush, and lace-edged handkerchiefs. All of these plus a half-tester bed with complete bedding and curtains, a marble-topped commode, a rush-upholstered side chair, a mirrored cupboard —all in light polished wood—and other items were found in a papered wooden chest labeled "Chambre de ma Poupée " and initialed "E. G." The original Paris department store price label appears on this charming chest with its lace-edged interior: "Au Bon Marché 10 F 50."

The initials "E. P.," incidentally, appear on the face of the gilded tin clock in the green sitting room (Plate 147) which ornate clock, with paper face missing, is identically reproduced on the dresser here, linking, along with the furniture in the French boudoir, all three rooms to the same manufacturer.

165 French Boudoir; *ca.* 1870; 8½″ high, 16½″ wide

Although the French room often, as Plate 147 demonstrates, folds compactly into a flat box, it may also be, as this sitting-room is, a permanent three-walled unit.

Very pink and white, this small room, smaller in scale than the quite similar bedroom is Plate 164, seems very likely an elegant lady's boudoir. Probably from the 'seventies, its gilded lead candle sconces are satisfyingly permanent. Such contemporary fixtures, along with the presence, nearly always, of the original wallpaper and draperies, are what make a miniature room so appealing from a historical point of view.

A liberty has been taken here, it should be recorded. The room's furnishings having been obviously incomplete (the round stool beneath the window at the right suggests the former presence of a piano or dressing table), they have been supplemented by a table and cupboard from a bedroom set of almost identical pattern purchased in the Paris Flea Market.

The brass album with scenes from the life of Napoleon and the ivory opera glasses with a view of "Le Monastery" in "Laghet" (Laghouat in Algeria) are among accessories which have been added. The trumpeting page perched upon the gilt clock and his fellow at either side comprise a set only recently brought together in one of those surprising reunions so satisfying to collectors.

166 1892 Paper Bedroom; size: 15″×16½″

Like the 1892 paper dining room (Plate 150), this bedroom, satisfyingly pristine, offers a complete portrait of its subject, from the turkey-red spread on the bed to the whiskbroom holder on the wall. The 'nineties are lovingly revealed in their peculiarly fussy detail. Not only is the aforementioned whiskbroom case be-ribboned, but it has even seemed necessary to tie a bow on the broom itself, not to mention the dresser bottles which are wearing jackets. The repoussé silver dresser set, the fringed towels on the towel rail, and the lifetime supply of dresser scarves on the dressers are other period details.

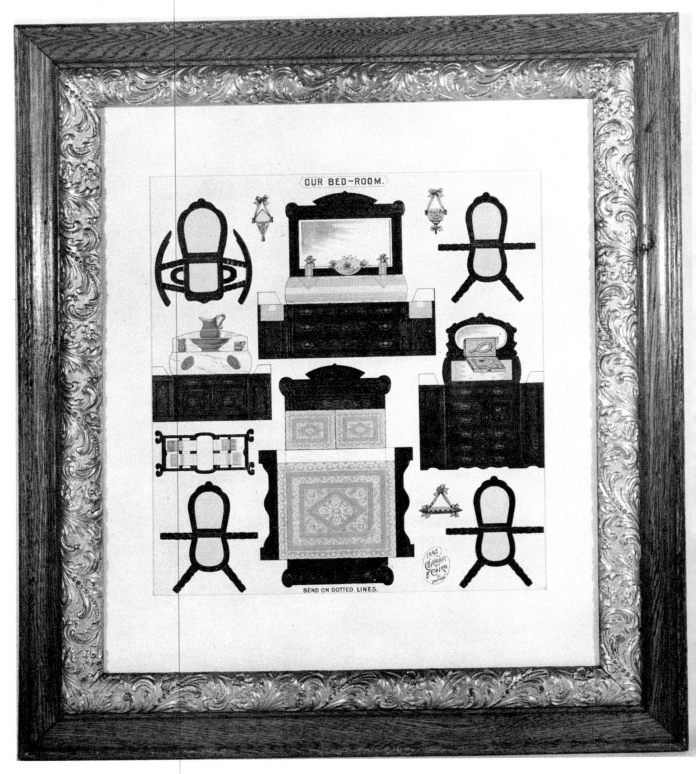

167 Fret-Sawed Bedroom; *ca.* **1880; 11½″ high**

In 1953, *The Spinning Wheel* in an article about "Fret Sawed Elegancies" detailed the evolution of the jig saw from the France of Louis XIV to its revival in the New York of one H. L. Wild. Beginning in the 1870's Mr. Wild did a land-office business in fret saw patterns, the saws themselves, and devices for animating such wooden wonders as steamboats, windmills, and fantastic clocks disguised as churches, workshops, and even locomotives.

For fanciers of gingerbread, there was no jig, jag, or curlicue left unsawed, and it is not surprising that this technique should have lent itself to Victorian doll houses and furniture. *The Spinning Wheel* reproduced Wild's line drawing of a fancy doll house, ca. 1880, and ten pieces of bedroom furniture.

A few years later, the set pictured above, almost identical to Wild's, was found in an Annapolis antique shop. The chest is two-drawer instead of three, and the design is not identical, but the forms are the same. The pieces are unpainted, of thin basswood about the thickness of popsicle sticks, and since they are fitted together with flat pegs, may be taken apart. The dresser has an oval mirror and brass bail handles on the drawers—accessories also available at Wild's.

An unusual feature of this set is an accompanying room with papered walls which fit ingeniously over the base and are attached by pieces resembling flat clothespins. Fret-sawed window frames in pairs, which are tacked to the walls with a layer of glass between, are the essence of everything a Victorian window should be. (The ones missing in the illustration have since been restored.)

168 Bedroom from the Tiffany House; mid-nineteenth century; 15″ high

In the Tiffany House, five pieces of furniture are believed to be contemporary, and three of these are in the bedroom—the tester bed with its original bedding and delicate silk bed curtains, the marble-topped bureau, and the commode. The fringed curtain on the latter is disintegrating with age, a ripe old age of at least a hundred years.

To these three rosewood pieces, a fourth has been added—a marble-topped dressing table. An ormolu towel rail with a fringed linen towel, a painted tin washstand with its original drapery, and on the bureau a brass watch-holder with a watch are further additions. The ormolu clock with its miniscule turrets and towers is made with unusual delicacy, and one wonders if the five blossoms embossed on its underside are some sort of manufacturer's mark.

169　A Variety of Beds

Perhaps, as Mrs. Greene has suggested in *English Dolls' Houses,* it is because the very small bed lends itself to home-crafting that doll house bedsteads of commercial manufacture tend to be in relatively short supply. Carefully upholstered in linen, many a small box with its lid placed at right angles to suggest a half-tester is to be found among more sophisticated furnishings.

Even so, the range of manufactured models is considerable, from the mid-century rosewood with its original, unmistakable, delicate silk (center) to the realistic, brass, tubular affair with removeable spring (bottom). Precise as a salesman's sample, the latter might have been suspected of such an origin had it not turned up—brass @$1.25; enamel @$.85—in F.A.O. Schwarz' 1910 Christmas catalogue (and still available in 1913). The writer once saw the identical bed, with the attractive addition of a brass half-tester, at an antique show. Also evidently of a series is the curious half-tester of black and gilt metal next to the rosewood example (right) since a similar bed, minus the tester, may be found in an English Early-Victorian House (Plate 117).

The rosewood half-tester, with its lavender gauze curtains in shreds and supported only by their sturdier lace edging, is a bed one might have expected to find in a mid-nineteenth-century doll house, but the folding type at the left is a considerable surprise to those of us who believed such contraptions peculiarly modern.

170 Miniature Plumbing; early twentieth century; 7½″ high, 13¼″ wide

Since from time immemorial bathing the baby has been an important and essential part of doll play, it is not surprising to find the plumbing-conscious twentieth century providing a complete bathroom in miniature—with running water.

This liquid, the one full-sized element always in proper scale, is provided, as in generations of tin kitchens before it, in small tanks above the basin, tub, and commode. Turn the basin tap, which *swivels,* and there is a wonderfully realistic plug on a chain to detain the precious fluid. There is also a roll for the bathroom tissue, a towel rack complete with towels, and that memento of a more precise era, the bath thermometer. But even more astonishing are the facts that the shower head has a pump arrangement in back which once provided at least an unsatisfactory shower and that the commode has a pull handle attaching to a tank above which, for all we know, may still be workable.

It is of interest to note that this "imported bathroom," to be had in "beautiful pink or blue shaded enamel finish," was pictured in the 1922 catalogue of F. A. O. Schwarz at a selling price of $6.00.

171 The South Jersey Bath; *ca.* 1895; 14″ high

It is probable that the South Jersey doll house (Plate 121) had no bathroom when it was made at mid-century, and perhaps the only liberty its owner has taken in its restoration has been to install one at the rear of the upstairs hall. The fixtures themselves are of the 'nineties or later. It must be remembered that antique plumbing abroad persisted years beyond our own and that toy furniture often lagged even farther behind the times.

The commode with tank above and pull chain is, of course, classic. A fixtureless wooden tub came with the curious shower structure, and we have taken a liberty in substituting the later model with fancy feet and brass faucets which turn. The "perfection" oil heater was a useful addition to a drafty bathroom, and the barely visible medicine chest above the lavatory and the shaving stand are other worthwhile accessories.

172 Appurtenances for Washing and Bathing

One of the most astonishing features of the first doll house on record—made for a Bavarian Duke in 1558—was a bathroom. Although public baths, beginning with the ancients, occurred in many eras, modern bathing was uncommon till after the Industrial Revolution. Even so, many country houses, writes an English historian (*A History of Everyday Things in England,* Marjorie and C. H. B. Quennell, London, 1933), were without fitted baths up to the end of the nineteenth century. A servant brought in a large bath mat and placed on it a large, low, circular tin tub with one can of hot water and one of cold. The bather sat or stood in the tub "and rinsed off the soap suds as best (he) could." Dolls had to cope with the same problem, and these tubs and cans, in shades of pink, blue, or green, may be found in many an English doll house. The ones in the foreground of our picture, in two scales, are here augmented by a pail and a hip bath.

The metal shower heads visible at the right rear plus the curiosity in wood in Plate 171 represent a style of bathing mentioned by Thackeray, in *Pendennis,* in 1850. Even earlier, in 1834, a shower bath which had been presented to Robert Burns was sold at the death of his wife. But the item found in miniature in the most infinite variations is the washstand with its inevitable accessory, the toilet set. The latter, consisting of bowl and pitcher (basin and jug!), soap dish, slop jar, sponge holder, pot, and every other essential, may be seen in metal, papier-mâché, and porcelain. The washstands themselves range from the filigree with mirror and metal, red-painted candles molded in (left) to the specimen with marble top and splashboard (lower right). The painted tin affair (center) has its original curtain and bow. The mid-nineteenth-century example to its left is metal painted to resemble marble. It seems essential to represent at least that ubiquitous accessory, the towel rack (upper right) with fringed towel.

Our detail picture shows plumbing fixtures from F. A. O. Schwarz' 1913 *Christmas Review.*

BATH ROOM PLUMBING FIXTURES

Wooden, white enameled.

Bathtub, 6 inches long	$1.00
Toilets	1.00
Washstands, Square	75c.

173 Cradles and Buggies

It is plain that lead filigree has a delicacy well-suited to nursery furniture; we note with surprise that most of the cradles we (rather absent-mindedly!) chose to photograph are of this gossamer stuff. The key to their survival must be found not in the fragile metal but in the number made.

The most glowing example, however, is not a cradle but a late-Victorian carriage—the one with parasol top (here anachronistically tended by a mid-century Nanny). A pressed-cloth-and-cardboard mattress to be found in the best-preserved specimens bears an 1893 patent date, and the buggies with and without their fragile parasols and in several scales are numerous. Actually, a Nuremberg firm still in business has been making filigree lead furnishings since 1799, but it is possible that these charming little carriages were made by the same manufacturer who turned out gross upon gross of soft-lead parlor sets for the 1893 Columbian Exposition.

Webster's definition for the article occupied by the bisque baby (below, center) is unexpected. His dictionary defines a gocart as "l. A framework on casters, to support children while learning to walk." We had hitherto suspected gocart only of his second meaning, "A baby carriage, esp. one with front wheels smaller than the rear wheels." By coincidence, a classic example of the latter is to the left of our bisque baby in the walker.

174 Dolls' Dolls and Toys

Like reflections in a series of mirrors, the doll's doll, then (possibly) the doll's doll's doll, growing progressively more infinitesimal, have their own special charm—not to be confused with that with which the Lord's Prayer is carved on the head of a pin, for the latter is a stunt or trick while the former is a steady progression. All doll house toys, including that most logical of all, the doll house's doll house, share this appealing possiblility of infinite diminution.

Here we have a girl doll with her dolls and a boy doll with his toys. The toys consist of three classics, a grocery wagon and horse of metal, a bicycle-built-for-two of lead, and a cup and ball of ivory. Most classic of all, the last, also known as bilboquet, has been a popular game since at least the fourteenth century. The ball, threaded to a cord, could, when tossed in the air, be caught in its cup or, with more difficulty, be speared upon the point of its handle.

The doll's dolls include a tiny early-nineteenth-century penny wooden fully jointed, a small jointed bisque, circa 1880, with miniscule wig, gingham frock, and black boots painted on, and that inevitable Victorian baby, the one-inch china Frozen Charlotte.

Part II: The Doll Houses & Shops **171**

175 Hall Furniture

It was undoubtedly because Victorian hall closets were so scarce that Victorian hall furniture was so plentiful. Several hat stands are shown herewith, the wooden one at the right sprouting realistic metal hooks. The imposing affair in the center with mirror and umbrella rack (seven hat pegs are regrettably missing) is interesting from another point of view. Trimmed with twigs, it is a miniature example of the mid-nineteenth-century preoccupation with the "picturesque," or more specifically, the style known as rustic. According to Frances Lichten in *Decorative Art of Victoria's Era*, "The 'rustic' manifested itself in two fashions; either it turned to the actual materials of Nature for its expression, or it imitated Nature's rugged motifs in any substance it chose."

Especially endearing in doll house scale are the small ormolu umbrella racks, in various styles, complete with umbrellas. The brass specimen at the left appears to be identical to one pictured (25¢) in F. A. O. Schwarz' Christmas catalogues of 1911–13. The gilded card tray, upheld by a muscular gilded boy, is relatively rare. The boy needed his muscles—in the later years of the nineteenth century, visiting cards were as numerous as snowflakes, and all of them together, as heavy as a substantial snowfall. In the earlier years, when visitors were rarer, cards were hoarded and displayed. Again according to Miss Lichten, "Here they were....available to the inquisitive who went through them, one by one—the direct if ingenuous method by which the Victorians used to gauge the social status of one another's visitors."

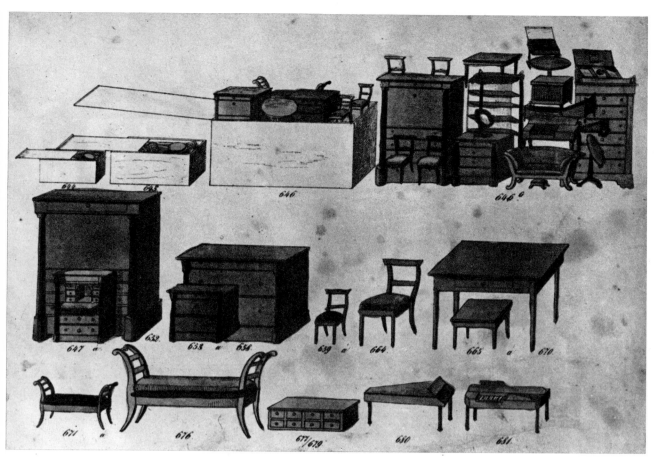

176 Miscellaneous Furniture in a German Toy Catalogue, *ca.* 1848

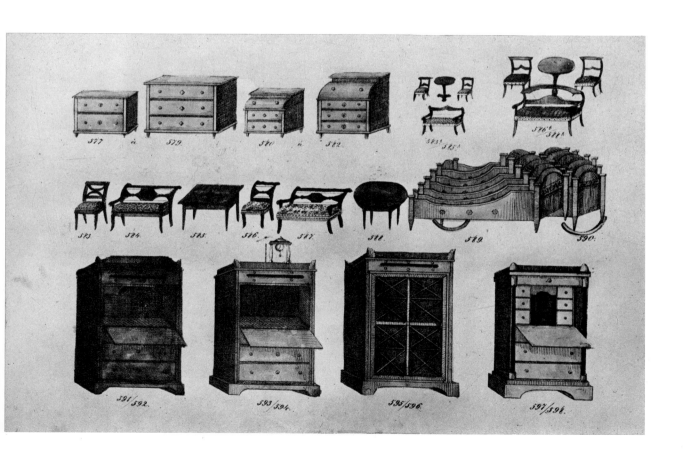

III The Domestic Arts

177 The Housekeeper's Lot

The housekeeper with her bunch of keys at her waist and the small maid with her feather duster here preside over a cross-section of the clutter of scrub brushes, buckets, feather dusters, brooms, carpet sweepers, beaters, and some of the other appurtenances with which housekeeping has been accomplished in the past. Victorian servants needed all such aids and more in an era in which storage closets were in short supply and bric-a-brac was triumphant.

"Probably no one article of modern invention and ingenuity has afforded greater satisfaction than wall-pockets." This challenging sentence is contained in a book about *Household Elegancies* published in 1876. Our example (left foreground), shown prone, is of gilded lead with a landscape across its tilted façade. We have also (not shown) several home-made versions in miniature, and these were plainly almost as important a part of the household of the past as the preceding statement suggests. According to Frances Lichten (*Decorative Art of Victoria's Era*), this was also called a "catch-all" and served not only to store "Grandpa's weekly paper" but also to protect housewives embarrassed by the intrusion of unexpected callers. The lady of the house, caught with dust cloth in hand, could tuck it quickly away! The red plush variation next to it holds a crumber and tray.

Again rather unphotogenically prone, the painted filigree metal object in the right foreground is a key cupboard, another customary accessory in the complicated Victorian household.

From a later era, the two vacuum cleaners, obviously early models, remind us that such electric cleaners in full-size were on the market as early as 1909. The toy makers kept pace: F. A. O. Schwarz shows a pewter "suction cleaner" for 25¢ in its 1913 Christmas catalogue.

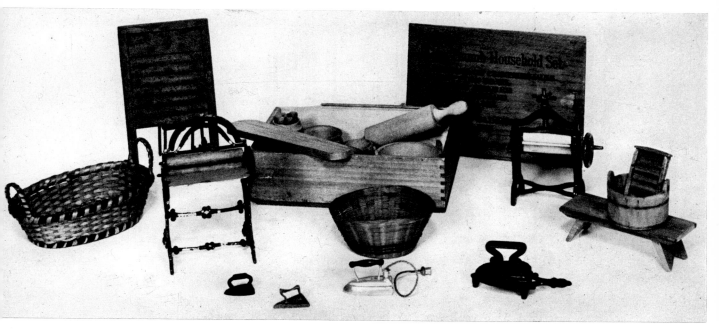

178 Laundering

Carpet beaters, wooden tubs, scrub brushes, flat irons, and trivets have been made in great profusion in several doll house scales. Early twentieth-century makers such as Arcade and Tootsietoy added washing machines with wringers and other more mechanical paraphernalia to the assortment. Since the electric washing machine in full-size had been on the market since 1905, the finding of early versions in miniature is not surprising. An Arcade model with wringer somehow eluded our photograph. As the illustration shows, the design of even so utilitarian an item as the mangle could unmistakably reflect its Victorian heritage.

179 Sewing

Especially miniature, and therefore particularly pleasing, are the small supplies meant for invisible stitches—the quantities of small objects for sewing a very fine seam indeed.

Of sewing machines alone, the variety is endless. The earlier ones, of soft lead, were obviously made in great quantities since, despite their fragility, a goodly number have survived. On these, the tiny treadle and the wheel are usually operable, and granted this wonder, if there is no needle to thread or spool to turn, who could dare to complain?

The small rosewood sewing tables with their lift-top compartments for implements and built-in pincushions are especially winning, and the implements themselves, irresistible, especially the scissors which may be found in various styles and nearly all of which cut. The ivory sewing set pictured on its original card includes the smallest of all thimbles and a stiletto for the elaborate punchwork embroidery done by our grandmothers. The pincushions shown, especially the beaded one, are probably more a dresser accessory than a sewing one, but perhaps they are dual-purpose. The most choice accessory, also a collector's item in full-size—and we have never even heard of another in miniature—is the sewing clamp with purple velvet pincushion on top which held a doll's fabric off the floor as she worked on it and prevented its becoming soiled!

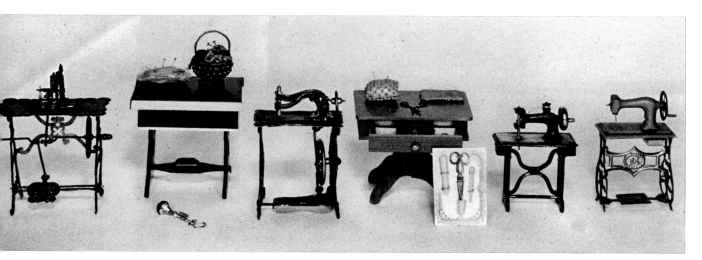

IV Heating, Lighting & other Conveniences

180 Heating

From the fine cast-iron grates, many of which were probably salesman's samples, to the soft-lead Victorian mantelpieces with built-in filigree fenders and even fiercely-painted lead fires, miniature fireplaces are to be found in a vast variety of metals and styles. Sometimes mantelpieces were part of a set of furniture, as in the painted tin parlor and bedroom suites advertised by a New York City toy maker in 1874 (See *A History of Dolls' Houses*). Considering how many doll houses had built-in fireplaces, it is remarkable how many of the latter were obviously made and sold as single objects.

The resulting profusion of accessories includes fine, early, polished brass fenders and fire tools of eighteenth-century simplicity and fussy metal filigree of surprising Victorian charm. Fancy stands of soft lead bristle with a battery of tools including the inevitable hearth brush, but a shovel and tongs often appear alone, ready to be propped against holders molded into either end of a soft-lead fender.

Coal scuttles, especially ones of painted tole with built-in shovels or glistening specimens in polished copper, tend to be enticing. So are metal and leather bellows and, for that matter, fringed hearth rugs.

When parlor stoves were fitted to fireplace flues in the middle decades of the nineteenth century, miniature ones were no exception. Some fancy shapes resulted, and we show several, as well as a supplemental heating unit which came later, the "perfection" oil heater, quite portable with its bail handle.

Inevitably, central heating came to the doll house at the turn of the century, here represented by two styles of radiators. The larger, "bronzed" one, in 15¢ and 25¢ sizes, was pictured in F. A. O. Schwarz' 1913 Christmas catalogue.

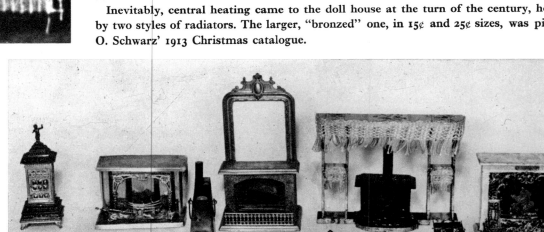

181 Candlesticks and Tables

Perhaps no miniature item is to be found in greater variety or quantity than the candlestick, in company here with its cousin, the candelabrum. In porcelain, glass, papier-mâché, turned wood, silver, ormolu, pewter, lead, brass, and painted tin, there is hardly a substance in which these are unrepresented. And the styles are even more diversified, from the red-painted tin chamberstick (foreground) with its extinguisher on a chain to the elegant blue and white porcelain candelabrum (center) with silver prickets, on which the candles were stuck, instead of sockets. (European pricket candlesticks were used as early as the twelfth century; the socket type which we use today did not become usual until the fourteenth.) Another unusual specimen, from France, is the brass push-up (left) with a ring which swivels the candle upward as it is revolved.

Among the random sampling of tables and stands, the mid-nineteenth-century parlor table (center), a variation of which was in the middle of every parlor, has its turtle-shaped marble mounted on a wooden frame exactly as the full-sized ones were. The smaller-scaled round marble-top (lower left), of the same age or a bit earlier, features painted lead dolphin legs, and the painted metal butler's tray (center right) has a soft-lead rail, "fringe" and legs, its sturdy surface decorated with a blue and white Delft-type scene of windmill, cottage, and landscape. Not shown is a matching plaque to hang above the tray. Dining room tables are not pictured either, but those with extension apparatus and matching leaves are small marvels of engineering.

182 Lighting: Lamps

Amongst doll house chattels, small lamps, especially Victorian ones with delicate Bristol globes crowning bases of glistening ormolu, are perhaps the most exquisite. Sometimes the shade is round; sometimes it ends in a roseate swirl. This pink embellishment may be seen on the third lamp from the right, front row, and on the one built into the small, tabled standing lamp in the rear. A lamp very similar to the former was shown in F. A. O. Schwarz' *Christmas Review* of 1913 in which brass lamps for doll houses were advertised at 10¢, 20¢, 25¢, 40¢, and 50¢. (See detail picture.) Sometimes there is a built-in chimney of clear glass, such as the one removed from the lamp at the left.

This lamp, incidentally, once had a workable wick, as did the tallest piano lamp, the globeless Victorian lady with upraised arm, and the large lamp with a frosted shade to her left. Most, of course, are "pretend," with kerosene only implied or the pointed electric bulbs of the 'eighties and later graphically suggested.

From the 1920's one finds working electricity. Shielded by a parchment shade, a small bulb screwed into a wood base may be lighted when the paper clip to which it is wired is attached to a small battery. We bypass this charming but somewhat clumsy type to show instead the bridge lamp (third from right, top), as evocative of the unmistakable 'twenties as a furnishing can be.

The Victorians are represented by piano lamps, student lamps, and table lamps. Quite unusual is the small filigree commode (center rear) with glass-globed lamp attached, the only one we have ever seen.

183 Lighting: Sconces

Obviously manufactured by the same toy makers who produced small lamps and chandeliers, doll house sconces are found in many similar guises. To the left, an oil fixture with a Bristol shade has a wick which lacks only fuel to illumine a doll house wall. When the sconce next to this was lighted, its two candlepower was doubled by the scrap of mirror, while the others pictured had to depend on the glitter of their ormolu shields for magnification. On the other hand, the two late-Victorian pointed electric bulbs required their Bristol shades to deflect the relatively great amount of illumination they produced.

Among the most appealing of doll house accessories are the small ormolu-type chandeliers with white Bristol globes which, to those of us who are addicted, have a jewel-like charm more alluring than that of diamonds. These add the ultimate touch to the Victorian doll house and may be found with three, four, or six gas globes.

It is interesting to note that the enterprising manufacturer, who may have found himself with a large stock on hand when electricity arrived, appears to have turned his glistening metal strands upside-down and substituted for his gas fixtures clear pointed bulbs (resembling Mr. Edison's earliest) with fluted white Bristol shades. This process seems to have been reversed in the case of one chandelier in the author's possession. Miraculously preserved in its original box, stamped "Germany" this bears a label which says "Elect. Chandeliers," with the "elect." crossed out. Since the fixture *is* gas, one suspects that this was boxed during the transitional period when both types were still available and that the seller had some sort of box or label shortage.

Another type of chandelier, of gilded lead, is less glittering, but *its* electric fixtures are suspended by an acrobatic cupid. A hanging lamp with one large glass shade, a hall type with a single small globe, and a range of earlier fixtures for candles, all to be found in innumerable variations, contribute to a remarkably detailed portrait of illumination in miniature.

Shown on the opposite page is a remarkable specimen with workable wicks.

V Decoration

185 Telephones and Thermometers

In the name of science, we unite two rather discrepant objects—the thermometer and the telephone. Although thermometers as we know them were invented in the seventeenth century, it was unquestionably during the late-nineteenth that they ceased being mere utilitarian devices for measuring heat and became articles of virtu as well. Leaving no object unembellished, the Victorians may accept the responsibility for the trio at the left. The modest item in pink celluloid next to the wall thermometer is from the 1920's. Enamored of the gilded lead lady with arm upraised, her maker, undoubtably German, also permitted her to preside over a clock and an oil lamp with wick, pictured elsewhere in this book. The small barometer on the mission oak stand is the only barometer we have encountered in miniature.

More recent is the history of the telephone, and that history is thoroughly represented in the doll house. No proper Victorian one is complete without that most intriguing of items, the wall phone with a bell on top which rings when the crank is turned. In about 1882, the transmitter or talking apparatus was separated from the receiver which was hung on a hook. In about 1890, the desk or standing phone was introduced, and this type is found in a number of miniature interpretations, including one in lead which may be seen in F. A. O. Schwarz' 1913 Christmas catalogue (detail picture). The modern French phone is also to be found in a variety of versions, and we regret that an early example, from Copenhagen, with a crank at the side arrived too late to be photographed.

186 Chairs I

To represent the innumerable patterns and styles in which doll house furniture has been made, perhaps no item can surpass that forthright household requisite, the chair. (The numbers following refer to the chairs in the order of left to right, beginning with the top row.)

Variations within a type are infinite. The Biedermeier chair with blue silk seat (1), for instance, may be found in a variety of scales, woods, and seat coverings and was obviously manufactured both in the United States and Germany. It may also be seen here (22), with arms and with delicate gilt stenciling both on the wood and on its glistening scarlet "leather" (oil-cloth?) upholstery, in an early but beautifully-preserved version. The gilt stenciling on dark wood occurs on two chairs of far less reserved style (13 and 15) lending support to the claim of English-doll-house historian Vivien Greene that a maker of such varied styles should be referred to as a doll's Duncan Phyfe. This seems a rather cumbersome, though charming descriptive, especially in view of the number of manufacturers who made similar pieces. "Rosewood," though a reference only to the material, may be sufficiently indicative, and Biedermeier is better still.

The wheel-back windsor with saddle seat (12) and the fancy chair (20), both from England and handwrought with the utmost delicacy, demonstrate along with such manufactured items as the bent-wood rocker (17) with its revealing profile unfortunately not shown, the Empire chair with ormolu mountings (19), and the tufted *fauteuil* from Belgium (8) how faithfully toy furniture reflected the productions by the cabinet-maker of full sized furniture.

Two interesting commemorative items are the Carver chair (9), a "Fac-Simile" of a chair brought over on the Mayflower by the first governor of the Plymouth Colony, and the ornate lead chair (16), which resembles no actual chair but is part of a set of sofa and chairs on which was impressed a scenic representation of the landing of Columbus, made for the Columbian Exposition of 1893.

187 Chairs II

Complementing our group in Plate 186, we offer another batch of what the *Britannica* refers to as "the most varied and familiar article of domestic furniture." Considering that for centuries the chair was largely an object of state and did not become common as a mere seat (replacing bench, chest, and stool) till the sixteenth century, it would seem that great progress in terms of variety was made in a relatively short time, in miniature as well as in full-size.

Perhaps, since Webster tells us that the chair is a "seat for one," the *confidante* at upper right is misplaced in this group and "conversation chair" (another of its names) is a misnomer, but we have taken a liberty and included this most Victorian furnishing, rendered here in brass and crimson silk.

An author of books about antiques, Carl Dreppard, who wrote one entirely about chairs, says that a *fauteuil* is an upholstered chair; Webster says a *fauteuil* is an armchair; and Larousse, who should know after all, agrees with Webster. Perhaps it is safe to say that chairs 2 and 10 are *fauteuils* since they fit both definitions, and these two were made, like the word, in France. Next to the latter is a chair (11) from a dining room set carved, in a wood resembling teak, in a Chinese style. (We have always been puzzled as to the origin of this set, of which we have seen one other, and would welcome clues.) With a seat and back of woven rush, chair 13 is one of a variety of styles made over a period of at least two decades of that endearingly delicate mesh.

188 Clocks and Watches

The clock, as much as any accessory, makes the doll house a doll home, lending a cosy, *gemütlich* aspect to miniature mantel or wall. If the doll house kitchen is the heart of the house, the doll house clock, minus tick or strike, is its pulsebeat. Its hands, forever folded at nine twenty-five or quarter-to three, are the only timepieces merciful enough not to remind us of the passage of time.

As our illustration suggests, the toy maker has by no means neglected this vital accessory. It appears in every guise, from alarm to tall-case, although, with the prevalence of the mantelpiece in Victorian households (the households most thoroughly considered in this volume), the mantel clock may be found in the greatest variety. The clock under glass bell occurs in porcelain as well as ormolu. One elegant specimen (fourth from left, top) combines both materials—a gilded figure, obscurely mythological, upon a porcelain pedestal.

On the left of this is a mirrored bronze example of considerably more recent vintage. This was available for 25¢ at F. A. O. Schwarz from 1911–13 and possibly earlier.* To the right of the porcelain and ormolu is a clock of equally specific date, 1876, in which year one E. A. Hotchkiss received a patent for, presumably, its pendulum which may be set into real and continuing motion by the slightest vibration. The clock just below it also does a trick, in this case when wound; the hands rush around its face to the tune of a loud ticking.

The two embossed brass watch holders with watches (foreground) are fetching. Before a Victorian gentleman retired for the night, he always hung up his pocket watch, and these two holders, one for the bureau and one for the wall, are miniature testimony to the contemporary belief that a watch ran better if maintained in a vertical position.

* See detail.

189 Pictures and Such

Like the full-sized walls they represent, Victorian doll house walls are thoroughly covered, and not only with fancy paper. In deference to the problems of photographing mirrors, we have omitted the charming variety to be found (with and without hat-pegs, candleholders, and other accessories) in miniature, but pictures are another matter.

"Art" came to the doll masses, as well as to the human, in the middle of the nineteenth century, and whether on walls or easels, there's a framed example of every sort to prove it. (In Plate 190 are illustrations of the sculptured variety.) Many pictures not expressly intended for dolls have found their way into doll houses. Miniature portraits such as the one of an ornately-framed Frenchwoman (lower left, oval), who looks suspiciously like Marie Antoinette, are an inevitable invader. This is signed "M. Poinsot." Just above her, what is believed to be one of the much-prized Baxter prints (from a color process patented in England in 1835 and made in sizes ranging from folio down to postage stamp) shows an elegantly clad party of ladies and gentlemen riding to the hounds.

But the most appealing of all are the pictures actually made for doll houses, again framed in the magical, non-tarnishing metal we've called ormolu and depicting landscapes, children, and other assorted subjects, charmingly colored. The oval at the bottom of the group is such a picture, as are the two above it. The latter represents that rustic conceit, the criss-cross frame, but here the boughs are interpreted in gilt.

Nearly every item pictured warrants a paragraph, but in the interest of brevity, we shall only allude to the embroidered silk mourning picture (lower right); the cork picture, a craft from the recently discovered Orient, above it; the triptych with children á la Watteau, which unfolds into mirrors (lower left); and two samples of the art of photography in easel frames to set upon the parlor table, a daguerreotype of Abraham Lincoln (left) and dual-framed portraits of German royalty. The stag's head, a very different genre, steals into this group by virtue of its status as a wall piece.

Shown in the detail pictures are a framed landscape and a mirror, from F. A. O. Schwarz' 1913 *Christmas Review.*

190 Bric-A-Brac

A fitting symbol of all she here surveys, Her Majesty the Queen—who gave her name to the whole fantastic era she represents—stands, a proud Parian figure upon her pedestal, amidst a small clutter of the knicknacks, whatnots, gimcracks, and articles of virtu with which that era was strewn. (Incised "R. Belt, 1897," this was plainly a souvenir of the Diamond Jubilee.)

Such a profusion had to be placed or encased, and the resulting variety of display cabinets, pedestals, and *étagères* is suggested here, with a folding screen or two for good measure, to fill any *unoccupied* space.

The chambermaid, who kept all these treasures dust-free, stands before a velvet-lined cabinet containing a complete breakfast set, from egg cups to coffee cups, in ivory. To the left of the folding screen in the Oriental taste so recently fashionable, a French mirrored cabinet in wrought iron, painted and decorated, holds bits of French porcelain.

A glittering ormolu *étagère* with mirrored back stands next to a wooden pedestal sold by G. A. Schwarz of Philadelphia, whose labels, fortuitously, appear to have great staying power. A bronze letter seal, found years ago in the Flea Market, is (somewhat dishonestly) mounted upon this one, but the other pedestals triumphantly bear toy statuary, except for the bearded gentleman upon the marbelized column at left, whose physiognomy, vaguely familiar, has not been identified to date.

Among the items in the foreground, of special interest are the amphora and jug (left), graphic examples of the classic revival, bronzes of Napoleon and Wellington (right), and a golliwog in Austrian bronze. Without these meticulously painted bronzes, may it be said, the doll house would be the poorer for potted plants, family pets, and objects d'art. That ubiquitous accessory, the glass bell, may also be noted here, with a religious figure within the example next to Napoleon and the traditional bride and groom on the brass corner stand at upper right.

The small fan of metal, in the foreground, looks very like the gilded palm leaf fan described by Frances Lichten, (*Decorative Art of Victoria's Era*), who pointed out that, "by the late 1870's Japanese fans . . . were solidly entrenched as reigning decorative royalties." They were wedged, she said, behind nearly every picture frame and mantel ornament—along with cat-tails and sunflowers.

191 Flowers and Potted Plants

Although bringing the outdoors inside is a peculiarly modern obsession, with a nod in particular to the picture window, cut flowers and potted plants are a bit of the garden which have invaded the house in all eras and thus inevitably have come also into the doll house.

The Victorians who could afford them had greenhouses and conservatories (Plate 197). With their love of bric-a-brac and clutter, they also had vases of every description, as every antique shop can attest, and although they sometimes filled them with peacock feathers and other items not entirely horticultural in nature and seemingly pressed any flower they could put their hands on, they also liked a lush bouquet. Empty vases may be seen in Plate 190. The two shown here which hold built-in flowers are a repoussé brass container in which another fancy of the period, dried grasses, has survived a remarkable number of decades, and a turned wooden doll house vase with a synthetic bouquet of doll house flowers in a similarly remarkable state of preservation.

To the Victorians, though, and to the Edwardians belonged, most earnestly, the potted plant. It is to our great regret that to date we have found in miniature no Boston fern, that long-ago standby of many a sunny window, but there is hardly another variety of plant that has not come to view. Many of these are by courtesy of that charming painted metal miniature, the Austrian bronze. A few pictured at random—holly, orange, daffodils, and bluebells—attest to their variety. Such exquisite miniatures are again being made in Austria, but the older ones, even with a bit of paint flaked off, are especially alluring.

Where there are plants, there must be plant stands. The mid-nineteenth-century, filigree lead, two-tiered affair (left) contains mossy foliage rather than pots, and the early "rosewood" example (center) supports its own wooden pots of fabric flowers, while the sturdy gilded metal specimen (right) holding no preconceived floral notion is here supplied with Austrian bronze pansies.

VI Pastimes & Pleasure

192 Music

The variety to be found in miniature pianos, square, grand, and, upright, is formidable. The early square pianofortes were made in several sizes, as shown; the tiny example (left foreground), five inches across, is obviously very early inasmuch as its black and white keys are reversed. The Smithsonian reports that such pianos in full size with keyboard colors reversed are from Germany or Austria and that all those in its own collection date no later than 1815. Since doll house styles lagged, the one pictured is probably somewhat later but has, as further proof of its antiquity, its gilt decoration hand-applied.

These charming little instruments coax gossamer wires to tinkle when their keys are pressed. Later pianos often contented themselves with paper keyboards, but occasionally contained music boxes which afforded key-wound concerts. One not shown plays "Three Blind Mice;" the imposing grand at the right rear, from the early twentieth century, thunders an insistent air not yet identified. A piano stool might also perform; the one behind the violin case winds up or down.

Schoenhut, whose numerous doll-size pianos, most of them astonishingly still in tune, continue to emerge from attics, put his celebrated name on the small, silent miniature at the right. Above it is a red cardboard grand with a candy-box top; pianos appear to have been a favorite conceit of Victorian confectioners, and the tall, early upright at the far left is also a candy box. The painted metal piano in the foreground has the charming addition of adjustable candle sconces.

Other instruments, including a cardboard violin in a straight-edged case from the turn of the century (right), are less readily come by. Like the ivory lute and the silver guitar, they tend to be cabinet pieces which have found their way into doll houses accidentally.

Musical accessories include gilt-embossed portfolios of "Musik," with *Wiegenlied,* or some other nostalgic treasure within, and prepossessing ormolu music stands. On the one at left rests a minissule, hand-written manuscript exquisitely inscribed by a mid-nineteenth century quill: *The Harp that Once through Tara's Halls.*

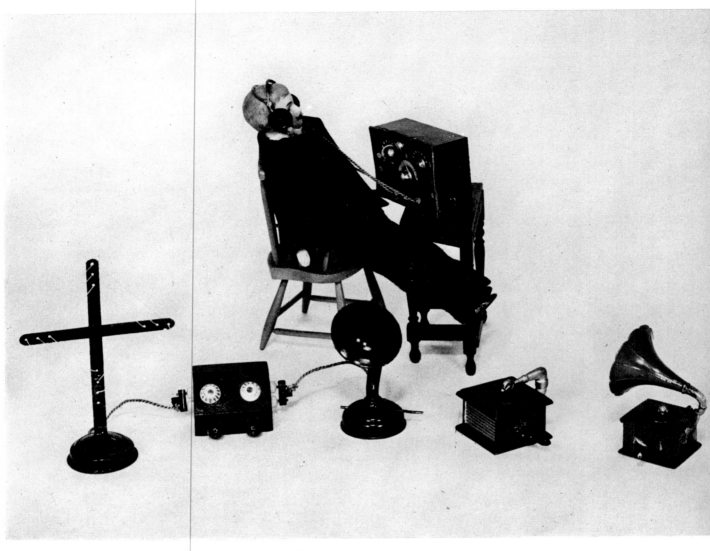

193 Radios and Phonographs

One was tempted to include a category called "modern inventions," but the stone-age appearance of this group of small marvels tends to belie such a heading. We let them stand alone, therefore, although the phonograph with morning-glory horn has some right to appear with the pianos and violins; when its crank is turned, scratchy "music" may be heard.

The radio at the left, from the 1920's, is complete with dials and tubes plus an aerial and loud speaker which may be plugged into small sockets in the cabinet. The ingenious German manufacturer also provided static; a small crank at the base of the metal speaker produces, when turned, a reasonable facsimile of this once-international noise.

The gentleman, of course, is listening to an earlier version of this remarkable invention, a crystal set with ear phones.

Of outdoor sports, winter appears to have the upperhand in our grouping, with snow shoes, ice skates, and a bob sled. The last is an especially detailed miniature; the brakes are workable with metal teeth to press into the snow when applied, and there is a rudder which obviously would steer, given a properly-skilled (and scaled) helmsman. The tennis rackets, of an early oval shape, reflect a young sport invented in England in 1874 which was all the rage a decade later.

Of indoor sports, checkers and playing cards are most often found in miniature, but it is rare to discover a Biedermeier table with its gilt checkerboard printed on "rosewood." Rarer still is the partial set of pressed cardboard checkers, black and green, tucked inside the drawer.

The tiny deck of cards (right) found in its original box has a four of hearts helpfully imprinted with the seller's name, "C. L. Wust, Frankfurt a M." Full-skirted ladies seated on the aces (in varying poses and scenery) as well as a lack of indices in the corners suggest a mid-century date. Numbers on cards became standard only after 1870; before then, the player had to count! However, this pack has turned up so often that one suspects a more recent vintage. Perhaps, like many toys, it remained in print, unchanged over a long period. However, with its delicate fernlike pattern on the backs of the cards, it fails in one particular which may qualify the plainer deck (left) as earlier. This one has not only the same absence of numerals but the cards also have plain backs. "The gambler's fear of being cheated prevented the use of decorative back designs until after 1850," writes a historian. "For it was felt that plain white backs could not so easily be marked." Playing cards have traditionally been made of pasteboard since only paste will make them properly opaque. The delicate white layer pasted on the back of each card in this plainer deck is apparent on several, even in miniature.

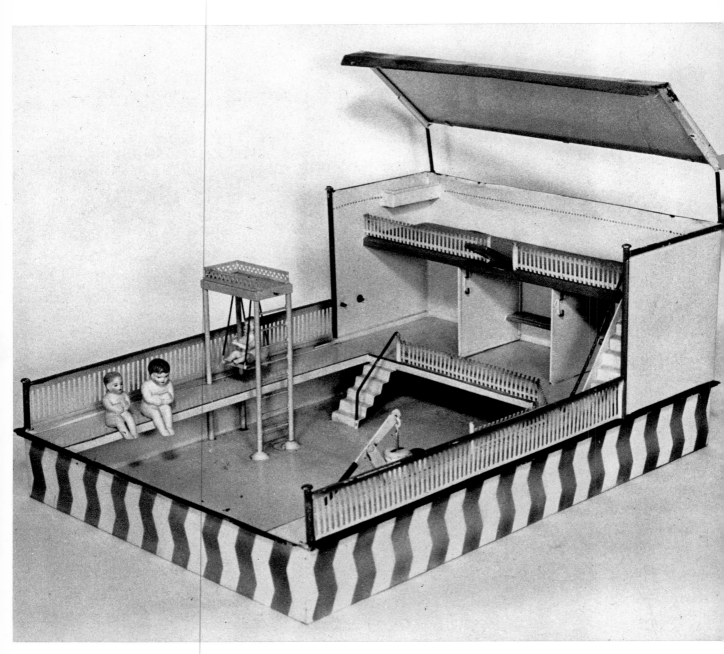

195 Swimming Pool

Although this metal swimming pool appears to be relatively modern, with its green, cream, and rust decor suggesting the early 1920's, surely no microscosmos would be complete without one example.

Scientific American in 1928 reported the manufacture of a doll swimming pool which had, among other things, a dressing room, diving platform, and a shower. "The shower has a miniature pump, operated by a lever," said the account, "which lifts the water from the main basin up to the shower head."

The 19″×14½″ pool pictured has no shower, but it lacks nothing else a well-appointed pool would require. There are two dressing rooms with built-in benches and clothing hooks, a sundeck with a removeable opaque glass canopy and diving board, a ladder to a lower diving platform from which a swing is suspended, and a workable pump. A sort of gargoyle is available to let in fresh water at a corner of the pool, and there are stairs protected by railings to all (presumably slippery) levels. The guard rails which rim the pool are a further protective touch. The small suitless bisque figures were present when the pool was purchased, but whether or not they were there originally is anyone's guess.

196 Luggage

Dolls tend to travel, as collectors of dolls from foreign lands can attest, and luggage therefore is a necessity. The well-turned-out gentleman shown here is surrounded by a supply that perhaps even the days of the Grand Tour did not require, but it tends to suggest the variety of trunks, valises, and hat boxes to be found in miniature. These were usually of cardboard and often the souvenir of a confectionery shop whose label still lines the interior. The pet carrier complete with pup is an example of the latter. The plaid steamer rug is a notable example of an era when one brought one's own.

197 Gardening

Where there are doll houses, there must be doll gardens. Although the garden pictured has been collected rather than planted, it offers some tangible evidence in support of this deduction.

One of two in the author's collection, the greenhouse shown has hinged glass sashes with small metal latches to prop them open in suitable weather. The benches within contain wooden pots of cloth flowers at the height of their bloom, and outside, cloth vines grow from small pots at either side of the doorway. The glasshouse not shown, of green painted tin with printed greenery, has a chimney and would, in England, where greenhouses contain only plants requiring no artificial heat, be known as a "hothouse." A young gardener's penciled labels still adhere to the brown wooden pots of wilted cloth flowers—such old-fashioned plants as thistle, moss rose, and blue bell.

Two trees, white birch and apple, of an indescribable substance but a remarkable realism were found in Germany. Not all the plants, in assorted sizes and pots, have been as well tended over the years as they might have been. One rather shaggy group has interesting clay pots, believed to be French, impressed with bands of pattern. The freshest of the plants, and the most exquisite, are the Austrian bronzes; a holly red with berries and an orange tree with fruit are especially beautiful.

A green-painted watering can, assorted rakes, forks and spades, and even a roller for the grass are present for the gardener's convenience; a painted iron garden bench is provided for the stroller's comfort. A most realistic metal lawn mower with wooden rollers is not shown with this group. It is probably, although the lawn mower was invented in England in 1830, of later vintage than this garden is meant to be.

Color Plate 12: Gazebo; **Late** Victorian; 14½″ high

No book embodying the Victorian house, toy or actual, would be complete without at least a reference to that small, decorative shelter known as the gazebo. This doll summer house, made in Germany (which is stamped on the bottom) has a blue-and-white striped awning for a roof and rose vines clinging to its thoroughly-turned posts. Within, a circular table and four chairs invite the visitor to a pitcher of lemonade or a glass of iced tea, and curiously, the table has a hole for an umbrella pole, suggesting that the manufacturer may have also supplied this as outdoor furniture minus gazebo and plus umbrella.

198 Pets

Since miniature animals have always intrigued collectors, it would be difficult to estimate the number of dogs and cats of bisque, bronze, ivory, and such at large in the world. Many of these animals have found their way into doll houses, making the size of the doll house pet population formidable.

Immortalized by the Victorians in painted porcelain as well as in actuality, that most Victorian of animals, the pug, is shown in our photograph, complete with puppies. A Boston Bull, sleekly accomplished in kidskin, and a fluffy white Persian, both with glass eyes, are similarly graphic representatives of an era. Since such playful conceits are unmistakable, the plaster pup with cigar, who has selected his stogie from the case at his feet, is plainly a Victorian type. Such whimsies are more commonly found in Austrian bronze in which a world of fantasy is exquisitely interpreted in painted metal.

Although "A Bird in a Gilded Cage" of the well-known song was a bird of another feather, so to speak, the pets who inspired the title are also redolent of the song's era, and the doll house interpretations of cages and birds are varied and numerous. Not shown in our picture is a cage in the shape of a house, imitative of a fancy to be found in full-size. The elaborate affair in lead filigree with its own fringed stand and the two ormolu hanging cages nearby house canaries, while the stand with perch accommodates a parrot. The small ivory cage is undoubtedly from the Orient.

Celluloid goldfish from the 1920's may be floated in the isinglass aquarium with its soft-lead stand (center); the painted metal goldfish rooted by metal stems to their house of real glass are undoubtedly earlier.

Worthy of note is the small pet carrier at the left, with its brown fabric cover, simulated leather binding, and small white dog behind its air-flap and grill. Like so many party favors which have found their way into doll houses (especially in the guise of pianos), this is a candy box, infinitesimal though the candies had to be.

Our detail picture shows a bird cage from F. A. O. Schwarz' 1913 *Christmas Review*.

VII The Shops

199 Early General Store; *ca.* 1800; 19″ high, 27½″ wide

Found in Zurich along with the toy stall in Color Plate 13, this appealing general store may be of the late eighteenth century, and is certainly at least early nineteenth. The labels on its sixty small drawers with bail handles are in German. A few are missing, and some are illegible; there are two styles, making one wonder if all are original. Figs, almonds, lentils, marjoram, caraway, candles, sago, and anise, at random, give a key to the type of merchandise they represent, and an expert in such items might write a learned treatise on the total.

There is a slot in the counter leading to a money drawer below and glass doors to display shelves behind the counter which is rather obscured in our illustration by the bead necklaces hanging in profusion. A net bag of attractive ceramic fish may be seen on the counter near one of two handsome baskets for sale with their original price tickets. Bundles of candles, a basket of coiled wax tapers, and jars of candy "pills" with stretched paper tops are among the stock. Fabrics were obviously a specialty of the shop. (Perhaps there was no mercer in the neighborhood.) There are shelves of tiny bolts, and although a museum authority on textiles has told us that they, actually cards of ribbon, are from the 1870's, considerably later than the shop itself, many are embroidered in lovely old colors and patterns and are late but delightful additions to this nice old store.

Color Plate 13: Toy Stall from Zurich; *ca.* 1800; 11″ high, 8″ wide

One felt indeed a Serendip when this toy and sweet stall from Zurich revealed its enchanting secret. Although its stock, about seventy miniscule toys and sweets, had been described as "of wood and plaster," the delicately molded fruits and figures felt too fragile to the touch to be of such heavy stuff as plaster. It was fortuitous that one tiny cupboard arrived broken, for a bit of paper neatly folded inside it reminded a momentarily distressed collector that this damaged treasure *had* to be of gum tragacanth, a substance which early-nineteenth-century pastrycooks combined with meal and sugar, molded into charming novelties with mottoes inside, and then painted. Printed in old German, the motto placed a century and a half ago inside the enchanting tidbit discovered here is as fatuous as most "fortune cookie" messages, but a treasure for all !that! It lead to the writing of *The Toy Shop Mystery* (Flora Gill Jacobs, Coward-McCann, 1960). Gröber, the German toy historian, tells us that the little figures were "for the most part edible" and became at their best an imitation of porcelain.

Among the meticulously fashioned articles in this collection are bowls of fruit, a little boy on his hobby horse, a mask for a masquerade, land the cuirass from a suit of armor. The wooden toys include checkerboards, bayonets, hobby horses, tenpins, whips, and tiny musical instruments, horns, drums, and lutes. The booth itself, which has a door in one side, is painted a rusty sienna without and a nice faded blue within and is presided over by a beautifully carved wooded proprietress whose face, alas, is missing.

200 Bull Butcher; *ca.* 1850; 13″ high, 12″ wide

Why the butcher shop should have a charm in miniature that it conspicuously lacks in full-size is demonstrated in this especially charming example with its quite uncharming sign: "Bull Butcher." The many little cuts of meat, realistic in shape, are quite unrealistic and chaste in material. The small roasts, sausages, and slabs of bacon are uniformly of a dark polished wood (bearing that patina so desired in antique furniture!) which banishes all thought of gore and reveals them largely as exquisite little objects. Especially appealing are two strings of link sausages. The meats, perhaps thirty-five in all, are hung by stout threads, darkened with age, on delicate hooks.

The value of old toy catalogues is well-illustrated, literally, in the case of this small butcher shop. Our description was presumably ready for the printer when the mid-nineteenth-century German toy catalogue referred to in the Foreword was discovered in Copenhagen. Because the shop sign was printed in English, it had been assumed that the shop was made in England where butcher shops were popular toys. Because a more specific dating seemed impossible, "Victorian" was the designation vaguely offered. With discovery of the catalogue, one of these assumptions has been clarified and one revised. As one can see, with the exception of a few bits of trim, the sausages, the ladder, and the butcher, this shop and the one in the catalogue illustration are nearly identical. Despite the English labels on this and the related poultry shop, fishmonger, and greengrocer (Plate 201), the catalogue is unmistakably German (see Plate 211 with German shop signs), and these shops obviously made in Germany for British and possibly U. S. import.

In the surviving shop, the sand is on the floor, and there are pegs where the butcher and ladder once stood. The footed wooden base of the structure, 11½″×6″, supports the yellow building with its red brick coigning and dark green roof. Stiffened net, covering two windows in front and one at each side, keeps flies from invading the proprietor's lodging upstairs. The meat, of course, is not so well protected.

201 Bull Butcher and other Toys in a German Toy Catalogue, *ca.* 1848

202 British Butcher; mid-Victorian; 16½″ high, 14½″ wide

Almost as traditional a British plaything as the toy theater, the miniature butcher shop may be found in varying degrees of splendor. Cooper Union Museum in New York City and Victoria & Albert in London have early Victorian examples crammed with roasts and haunches in which hardly a rib or vein is left undefined. These are quite beautiful and examples of Mr. A. C. Benson's theory, charmingly elaborated elsewhere, that "there is great beauty in smallness...the blemishes and small deformities...all disappear."

A fetching but more modest example of the British butcher shop may be seen in our photograph. This one has the addition of the butcher's living quarters above. The butcher, a chalkware fellow, wears his top hat, as a proper butcher should, but his cleaver is missing, an absence indicated by the empty scabbard at his waist. We know that he's been standing in the same spot for a century or so inasmuch as he fits on a peg near his doorway. Little was left to a child's imagination in Victorian days, but antiquarians may rejoice here at the permanence of a position as well as an object.

203 English Grocer's Shop; Victorian; 15″ high, 28½″ wide

This attractive Victorian toy had been part of an English collection of toys and games assembled in the early years of this century and packed away till recently. Undoubtedly it is of considerably earlier vintage than this history implies. There is evidence that the shop was thoroughly played with for years before, even though some of the accoutrements are of a later date. Bits of trim are missing, and the only clue to the original blue pattern of the wallpaper, now faded brown, is to be found under a hanging shelf at one side. The style and detail of the woodwork also indicate an earlier date than the likeness of Edward VII on an attractive red, gold, and blue tea canister, or even that of Her Majesty Victoria on an embossed flat tin box dated 1900, would suggest.

Porcelain labels on the drawers mention "Candy" as well as such foodstuffs as "Flour," "Rice," and "Cocoa." The two metal urns in niches alongside the drawers and the wooden kegs in a rack on the floor promise beverages brewed on the premises. Appealing items on the shelves include a wooden case imprinted "Boot Buttons Penny Per Box" and a sponge with a price tag marked "7½d." A wooden rack on the counter may once have held an account book. The roll shutters still glide smoothly outside the glass windows.

Color Plate 14: Gertrude's Store; *ca.* 1880; 18½″ high, 23″ wide

Although the two stenciled placards proclaiming that this is the "Kaufhaus" of "Gertrud" are an addition, this pretty shop is largely in mint condition, suggesting that its small owner was careful with her toys. The sixteen drawer-fronts with their imitation wood veneer and their brass labels proclaiming the usual staples and spices (Biscuit and Salz, Safran and Anis, and Lorbeerb I., which seems a roundabout way to abbreviate bay leaf) are like new. Perhaps the yellow wooden frame and its red applied-trim have been repainted, but with its handsome glass windows at front and sides and its scroll-cut embellishments, this is as appealing a doll's shop as one might wish to see.

It is possible that the half-dozen potted plants, also as fresh as daisies, and some of the other fittings, are additions. The plants are quite small in scale for the rest, but there are often discrepancies in scale in shops, and also in kitchens. Here, one of the most interesting fixtures, which has to be original because it is attached to the counter, is the scale, a mammoth object which virtually covers the counter. Four niches contain the weights.

A pair of hinged, painted tin cake boxes, several tea canisters handsomely decorated with scenes of life in the Orient, a few pieces of stoneware and glass, and the visible assortment of porcelain jars are among the shop's varied containers.

204 Cardboard Grocer; Victorian; size: 15¼″ × 19¼″

We have alluded elsewhere to the pristine satisfactions of uncut cardboard furniture. But given the complexities of a French grocer's shop, ca. 1870, in precise historical reproduction, the rewards are boundless. This hand-colored sheet by Pellerin ("Imagerie D'Epinal, No. 355") is so crowded with minutiae that it is hard to see how it could possibly have been cut and glued by a magician, much less a child. But left uncut upon its sheet, it is a detailed portrait of a French grocery of the day, and no one attempting to assemble a Victorian shop of any kind can fail to benefit from studying the bins and crates and bottles.

Ripainsel was the name of this grocer, we learn from his sign, and he dealt in "Eau-de-Vie & Liqueurs" as well as "Epicerie & Mercerie." Monsieur himself, in visored cap, green coat with sleeve protectors, and long apron, stands, ready for a scissor which has resisted him for nearly a century. A delivery boy with bottle and parcel, an elegantly garbed matron whose vast bustle seems hardly capable of weaving through the vast merchandise, and a maid-servant and young girl, each with a pitcher brought for filling, also wait patiently upon the page.

There are strings of sponges to hang, shelves of brushes and blue sugar loaves to affix, and a scale to assemble and set in the center of the marble-topped counter. It is an absolutely disarming sheet of cardboard.

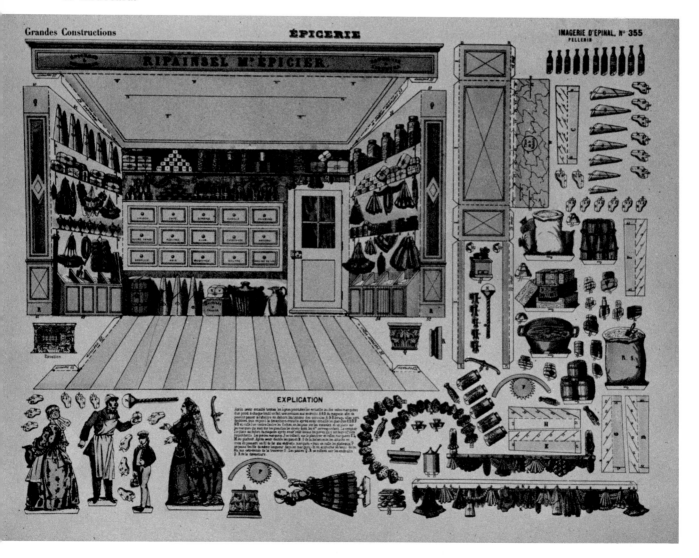

205 Small Grocery; Victorian; 7¼″ high, 16″ wide

Found in almost perfect condition, the freshness of its maroon wallpaper and its brown and white flooring intact, this modest toy with its stenciled paper-over-wood counter and its porcelain drawer labels shows with what taste we honored our children in the pre-plastic era.

The stock of lanterns, jugs, and rubbers has been added, as have the scale and the mouse.

206 Dutch Delicatessen; *ca.* 1900; 15″ high, 22″ wide

It is interesting to observe that this shop, though less elegant in purpose and decoration, is strikingly similar to the milliner's shop in Plate 208 and obviously was made by the same manufacturer. The design of the counter and a number of embellishments are almost identical.

Labeled in Dutch, a surprising supply of small tins still stock the shelves. It is likely that labels in other languages for export to miscellaneous countries were made by the same factory. In an occasional miniature shop, one sees labels on similar tins printed in several languages to serve an assortment of countries. One grocery in the author's collection uses the international language—a picture of the product, with no lettering.

The small shop pictured has unfortunately been repainted (even the tins have been silvered in a stubborn paint which resists all efforts to remove it), and it appears to have been "restored" by an adult who may have used it as a display piece, possibly in a shop window in the Netherlands where it was found. "W. D'Oliphant" has been lettered under an ebony elephant perched at the top, above the original "Delicatessen" label.

But aside from these alterations, its stock is remarkably complete. A wall telephone, possibly added by the owner, hangs in a rear alcove next to the mirrored door. The built-in drawers are labeled, in metal, for such unmistakable stuffs as "Chocolade" and "Thee," and other merchandise includes the traditional blue sugar loaves, a package of green sealing wax, and the thimble-sized tins which bear such labels as "Haring," "Ragout von Tong," and "Astrakan-Caviar."

207 Grocery with Office; late Victorian; 9¾″ high, 20½″ wide

This appealing grocery was found in remarkably unblemished state, with the unfortunate exception that its counter was missing. The temporary substitution (from an incomplete grocery, undoubtedly earlier, found in Nuremberg) is believed to be similar, as suggested by the drawer's resemblance to the surviving original drawer alongside.

The intriguing feature, of course, is the proprietor's office, separated by its own door and provided with a shiny brass bell which rings clearly when the handle in the shop is pulled. Also present are the proprietor himself (a bearded chalk figure), his wooden desk, and a variety of wooden canisters with such arresting labels as "Prussian Snuff."

208 Victorian Milliner; *ca.* 1900; 18″ high, 27½″ wide

As though the pristine condition of its mirrored cabinets, its blue and gilt decor, and its enchanting accessories were not disarming enough, this lovely toy bears a further collector's delight—its original label. When the celebrated New York toy seller F. A. O. Schwarz helpfully affixed his name and address, the latter was "West 23rd Street," the firm's location between 1890 and 1910. Although a twenty-year span will seem rather wide, it is relatively specific in the dating of toys where designs were frequently repeated for several generations. The styles of the delicate felt and straw millinery, be-flowered and be-plumed, which stock the shop may be a bit later. Presumably all the merchandise came with the shop, but one cannot be positive.

The counter, a pair of wide drawers behind it, and the elegant pair of console mirrors at either side which hang upon the delicately papered walls are movable. Other original accoutrements include the delicate metal hat display racks, weighted and gilded, an ivory hand mirror, and a standing wooden hat rack. The bisque clerk and customers and a cash register (National) have been added. The latter, a bit later in vintage than the rest, should probably be bronze rather than silver to be properly "period."

It is interesting to compare this shop with the Dutch delicatessen in Plate 206 which has many similar details of design and is obviously from the same maker. Another in the series, even more striking in its contrasts, may be seen in F. A. O. Schwarz' 1910 circular. This is a butcher shop, an establishment one could not imagine further in spirit from a milliner's, especially such a rococo one as this, but virtually the same framework, with identical clock, counter, and columns may be seen in the illustration, with meats on hooks replacing the hats on stands. Other accessories included block, wall phone, scale, and the butcher himself, and the sizes ranged from a shop sixteen inches wide at $1 to one twenty-eight inches wide with "side room" at $6.

209 Grocery from F. A. O. Schwarz; early twentieth century; 16½" high, 28" wide

Like our milliner's shop in Plate 208, this attractive grocery store has the additional allurement of an F. A. O. Schwarz label on its underside. The only disadvantage to this label is that the address printed thereon, "Fifth Avenue at 31st Street," was Schwarz' between 1910 and 1931, causing us to attribute a later date to the toy than we might have otherwise. By its style, it appears to have been made, undoubtedly in Germany, before World War I, but obviously not much before.

In surprisingly good condition, with its metal drawer labels bright and its canned goods in abundant supply, an ingratiating feature are the paper labels on the cans—pretty fruits in color with no lettering to impose a language difficulty upon miscellaneous importers. Painted ceramic insets embellish the stenciled counter and shop frame.

A grocery store which is nearly identical, differing only in minor, mostly-decorative details, is shown in F. A. O. Schwarz' 1910 Christmas brochure. This has an extra row of drawers at the top, instead of the open shelves, and shelves at the back, instead of the door. This was evidently a popular item; in the 1913 Schwarz catalogue, nine different styles were available in various sizes and styles ranging from a simple affair twenty inches wide at $1.75 to a twenty-eight inch emporium "very complete" at $16.50. A grocer dressed in a dark business suit is shown in the illustration of, presumably, the latter store.

It is interesting to note that this same store (with only one apparent variation, two counters instead of one) was still to be seen in the 1920 Schwarz catalogue—a significant comment on the number of years almost identical toys were often made and the difficulties of dating them precisely.

The unusual stall with mirrored counter and workable striped awning is pictured here to emphasize an interesting detail. The metal drawer labels are identical to those used in the store and suggest that this attractive piece was probably from the same maker. It is eighteen and a quarter inches tall.

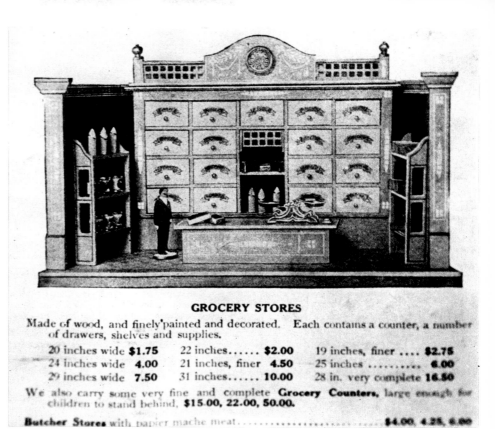

GROCERY STORES

Made of wood, and finely painted and decorated. Each contains a counter, a number of drawers, shelves and supplies.

20 inches wide **$1.75**	22 inches...... **$2.00**	19 inches, finer **$2.75**
24 inches wide **4.00**	21 inches, finer **4.50**	25 inches **6.00**
29 inches wide **7.50**	31 inches...... **10.00**	28 in. very complete **16.50**

We also carry some very fine and complete **Grocery Counters**, large enough for children to stand behind. **$15.00, 22.00, 50.00.**

Butcher Stores with papier mache meat.................................. **$4.00, 4.25, 6.00**

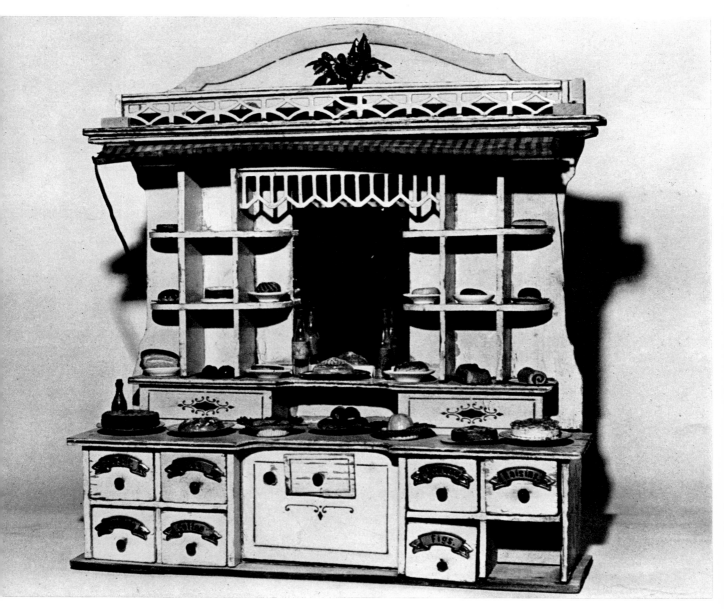

210 Late Butcher Shop; early twentieth century; 6½″, 13″ wide

A number of these small butcher shops, simple affairs compared with the crowded ones of an earlier era, were found in mint condition by a Baltimore antique dealer a few years ago. The blue and white pattern of the paper floor and the red and gray walls are a neat background for the simple wooden counter and the suitably detailed composition cuts of meat which hang by hooks from brass rods across the back. From the same old store stock, small tin scales were found in quantities and one placed in this shop.

211 A Page from a Toy Catalogue, *ca.* 1848

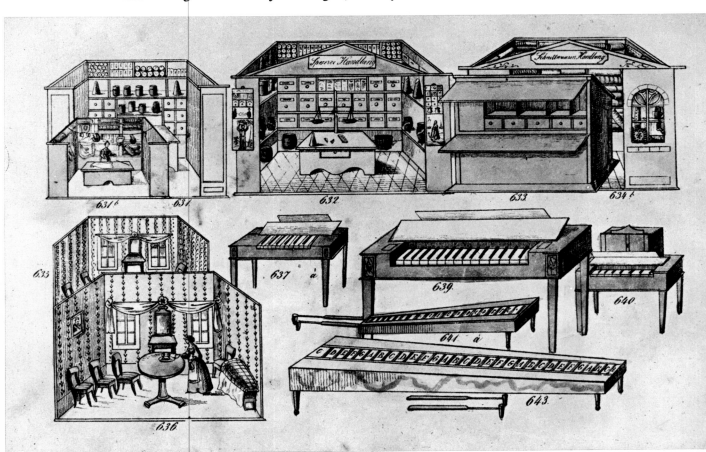

Color Plate 15: From the Shops

As a footnote to the shops pictured, we offer a small cross-section of the alluring items to be found therein, including a customer.

A weighted gilded hatstand complete with hats, from the milliner's shop in Plate 208, speaks for itself, as does the scale, one chosen at random from a bewildering variety. The single canister with Edward VII on its lid and such choice British subjects decorating its sides as a jack-tar dancing a hornpipe and a Scottish Highlander performing a sword dance is from the British grocer's shop in Plate 203. The three cans of fruit (from the grocery in Plate 209) bear labels on which their contents are pictured. There are no printed words to impose a language limitation on those who import them.

Unusual items from an outdoor market whose baskets of produce were unfortunately dispersed before the present collector came upon them include the paper poke on which the name of this dismantled shop is printed. Freely translated from German, this reads "Brothers and Sisters Store. Delicatessen. Fruits from the South and Wine." The fragile poke is one of a sheaf in several colors. Equally intriguing is the wire mesh till with compartmented metal tray loaded with tiny coins, the smallest three-eighths of an inch in diameter. These appear to be copies of actual German coins, and many are dated "1910." Some have embossed profiles of Kaiser Wilhelm with his name and title spelled minutely around the rims, and even the metals represented are similarly realistic, having the appearance of silver, copper, and gold.

212 Dolls' Antique Shop; mixed vintage; 16¼" high

"There is great beauty in *smallness*," A. C. Benson wrote in the wonderful book about Queen Mary's Dolls' House. These words go far to explain the preoccupation of so many adults with model trains, planes, boats, dolls, and houses. Doll house history is as full of adults as of children and, if the element of choice be considered, possibly fuller.

From London, the miniature antique shop pictured was obviously made by an adult for his own pleasure; how recently, it is not clear. The small bisque proprietress is not nearly as old as most of the merchandise, but then, it is an *antique* shop. In any case, it has been accomplished with flair and charm, and there are some fine bits of treasure on its counter and shelves.

Crowned by a luminous picture on glass of the Crystal Palace Exposition, the shop has a set of shell furniture—chairs, a table, and a settee—with blue cotton upholstery even on the table top. On the crimson velvet counter dominated by four splendid pieces of statuary (especially splendid, the Tars in their middies and whiskers), there are the most astonishing smidgins of craftsmanship and charm: a framed diminishing mirror the size of a farthing, an oval of fine Florentine mosaic, several examples of punched leatherwork, an ivory-handled razor, and an ivory cup and ball for the ancient game of bilboquet. Choice curiosities of carved ivory may be found throughout, along with wooden butter-molds and paper crests and seals. Evidently cut from letterheads, these crests are surprisingly decorative in multiplicity, whether representing "St. John's College, Cambridge" or simply an otherwise anonymous "Harriet."

Many souvenirs of mid-nineteenth-century England—and Empire—a lacquered plaid knife box stamped "Caledonia" (a reflection of the royal family's preoccupation with tartans), a pierced brass box from India, and a shell painted with roses by the hand of some patient British seaman, are interlarded with such diverse items as Nevers glass dogs with bulging eyes, a fringed French doll parasol, and hanging from the rafters, a crystal chandelier.

VIII Stables, Schoolrooms and such

213 French Schoolroom; Victorian; 8″ high, 18½″ wide

A charming lesson in French geography, this small schoolroom has on its blue walls delicately colored maps of four French departments with sketches of scenic and historic attractions surrounding each. In the department of Ille-et-Vilaine, we are shown the tomb of Chateaubriand, the Cathedral at Redon, and the Hotel de Ville at Rennes; in the department of the Basses Alpes, the ruins at Digne, among other sights; and in the departments of Yonne and Drome, similar wonders.

The little schoolroom is in the style of all French doll rooms which do not fold entirely; with its folding floor flap, it becomes part of its own deep box for storing. A metal clock marked "H. H. Paris" has been substituted for a wall clock previously removed. Liberties have been taken with the addition of such non-French but irresistible accessories as a German atlas with colored maps of the continents, red "school-bags" containing note books with precisely realistic black-and-white marbled covers, and cardboard slates with crumb-size sponges attached. The school desks with lift tops and attached seats and the blackboard which shows signs of thorough use are original.

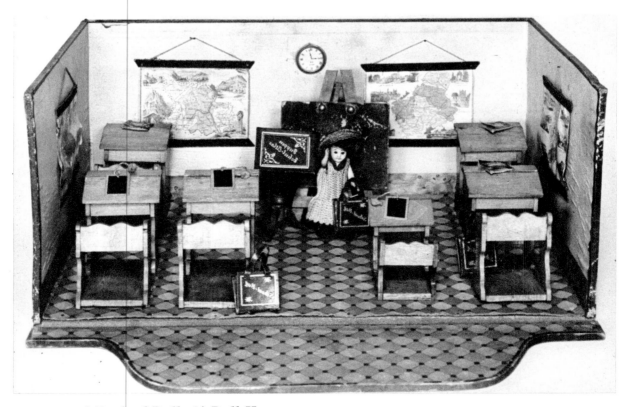

214 Folding Schoolroom; Victorian; 8¼″ high, 12″ wide

The folding cardboard walls, printed with two simple windows, fit into slots in the wooden box-lid of this delightful schoolroom. The blackboard and desks with attached benches are, like the schoolmaster's bench and stand, of painted wood.

Himself of painted composition, the gray-haired schoolmaster teaches an intriguing group of students, all of whom are carefully woodcarved and artistically painted. The "student body" is dressed in maroon, brown, or blue with white embellishments, the girls' outfits including matching cotton skirts below their wooden blouses. Both boys and girls have jointed wooden arms and legs, the latter with black boots painted on. Each literally sits on a tack, a small prong in the figure's posterior, but may easily be made to rise to answer a question or to leave the room.

We recently saw, in a small glass case substituting for a schoolroom, a similar professor, blackboard, and students. The school desks and the professor's lectern were identical in style, but of stained rather than painted wood, with no inkwells indicated as they are on these.

We do not know where these charming toys were made, though the Tyrol may be suspected.

215 Lithographed Stable; Victorian; 20″ high

Since nearly every Victorian house had a stable, one expects to see in miniature almost as many stables as Victorian doll houses. As it happens, the number appears to be considerably smaller, but a variety may be found.

The one pictured is unusually choice, a sizeable affair consisting of four stalls and a hayloft above. The gate to each hinged stall fastens with a metal catch similar to the ones on Bliss houses. So many details, incidentally, are similar to those found on Bliss houses that one wonders if this stable could have been made by Bliss. The metal railing on the stalls, balconies, and hay bin is identical to that used on at least one Bliss house (Plate 131). The lithographed paper-on-wood columns are almost identical in design to smaller ones on the same Bliss house. But amongst the lithographed profusion of scrolls and orange and blue embellissment, the Bliss name is nowhere to be seen. The only printed clues are numbers ("624 K" or "624 E" etc.), obviously to guide bits of lithography to their proper destinations.

Two leather horses and a wooly one of dubious origin were the only inhabitants of this fine stable when it was acquired.

Our detail picture, from Schwarz' 1913 *Christmas Review,* shows an attractive stable and reveals, in the fine print below, what an astonishing variety of stables was to be had before the automobile vanquished these toys forever.

WOODEN STABLES
With Papier Mache Horses

No. 5232 2 horses and wagon with hay-loft, 14 in. wide............$2.50		
No. 5384 2 h. and wagon, with stairs leading to hay-loft. 18 in. wide. 4.50		
No. 5393 4 h. and wag., doors, hay-loft, 24 in....................... 6.00		
No. 5395 3 h. & wag., doors, stairs leading to dwelling on 2d floor, 24 in. 8.00		
No. 5388 Similar to No. 5395, but larger, 33 in.................... 12.00		
Stables with skin horses..............10.00, 12.00, 15.00, 20.00, 25.00		
Stalls with skin horses........................10.00, 12.00 and upwards		

216 No. 2 Fire Station; early twentieth century; 17″ high

No microcosmos would be complete without a fire engine house; the peril of miniature conflagrations to miniature houses can never be far out of mind. No. 2 Fire Station bears a family resemblance, in style and scale, to the Bliss houses, though there is no Bliss name to be found helpfully upon it. Since such brightly lithographed paper-over-wood buildings came from Germany as well as the United States, one cannot be sure, even with the wording in English, that this is not a German import.

Lithographed on the upstairs windows ("hanging" inside) are such appropriate items as firemen's helmets, boots, outercoats, and even a speaking trumpet. "Through" the downstairs windows, the same round steam boiler may be seen that is more three-dimensionally represented on the rear of the toy fire engine standing in front of the station. This friction toy, an addition, shoots sparks and makes siren sounds as it races across the floor. With its 1912 license, it is probably later than the fire house. The leather Dalmation with glass eyes is also an addition but, of course, a traditional one.

For a toy otherwise made with so much detail, it is amusing to discover, when the building front is swung open, a conventional two-room wallpapered doll house interior within. There is not even so much as a brass pole for a fireman to slide down.

217 From the Japanese; mid-nineteenth century; 18″ high

The beautiful and ritualistic doll displays which, on March 3 of every year for centuries past, have been the focal point of Japan's Girls' Festival are, of course, often larger and more elaborate than this one. Some of these family treasures, handed down from generation to generation, have required a sizeable room for display, but the petite company pictured here within its own small case is one of the most charming examples we know.

It has, as it must, the essentials of the *Hinamatsuri*, especially the *dramatis personae*, with a few attractive embellishments. There are, of course, the inevitable shelves draped with red cotton cloth, and on the top one a court noble and his lady are seated. Three lesser court ladies grace the second shelf, and a singer and four musicians with flute, drum, and tambourines are on the next. The fourth shelf supports a military and a civil dignitary, the military man with his sheaf of arrows slung upon his back. Three male servants are last, on the lowly fifth shelf between the essential blooming orange and cherry trees. Other miniature accessories, lanterns, lacquered boxes containing offerings, and tea services on low tables, are traditionally dispersed among these plump little personages in their padded brocades. Their delicate plaster faces gaze inscrutably.

218 Zoological Garden; *ca.* 1908; (average figure) 2¼″ high

A related toy in the microcosmos of doll houses is the lead or tin village or zoo. This attractive zoological park, with its lead animals, edifices, personages, and vegetation neatly painted in pleasing colors, is probably German-made. The dress of the visitors who stroll beneath the trees or sit on the benches very specifically suggests the year this menagerie was created—1908 or thereabouts.

The passengers on the pony cart, bench, and horse-drawn streetcar may leave their appointed stations, though they would be obliged, it is true, to go about in rather a crouching position or to lie, knees drawn up on the grass! The seal may be parted from his rock with less embarrassment. The most intriguing example of detachability is the hat on one of the ladies, which may be removed if the day is warm. Possibly the other hats have been glued firmly in place, since an exception would seem unlikely. The various gentlemen, including the driver of the horse-car, exhibit a variety of moustaches and whiskers as carefully indicated as the camel's humps and the zebra's stripes, and much more revealing of era than the latters' more traditional garb.

219 Miscellany of Objects

Presided over by a Victorian gentleman (since many of these articles are of a gentlemanly nature), herewith is offered a small assortment of objects which help support the author's thesis that "almost everything which has ever been made in full-size has also been made in miniature."

The gilded and embossed soft-lead medicine chest with workable latch and, within, its "Wadding," "Pills," "Fennel," "Spirit," and "Oil" is as specific as the soft-lead typewriter with its rubber platen into which, courtesy of a tiny crank, paper may actually be rolled. A later model, in which three small keys may be pressed to strike a crumbling (probably original) page, is disarming in a different way.

A gentleman may also find useful the shaving stand with mirror and brush, the gout stool, the cigar cutter, the cigar (!), and the meticulously made tools including hammer, plane, saw, and miter saw. The last two will operate with precision on any matchstick or toothpick.

If the gentleman is in business, he will also appreciate the lead cash register with its four keys which, when pressed, cause 1, 5, 10, and 50 to pop into better focus behind a glass panel. A crank also animates these keys and numerals, and a drawer below holds gilt coins embossed with animals. "Ihre Zahlung" is embossed on a plaque at the top, with "Amount Purchased" on the back. For American import, undoubtedly, the positions have been reversed. (Later American models also have "National Cash Register" embossed above the keys.) Like the first cash register, invented in Ohio in 1879, this one, very different in appearance, does "nothing but indicate the amount of a sale on a dial" *(Britannica)*.

Also shown are an ice water cooler, a lead filigree hanging key cupboard with four hooks behind its gaily decorated door, a painted metal hanging lavabo (rather foreshortened by its prone position), and a plaid ottoman with velvet top. From an early-Victorian English doll house (Plate 117), the ottoman has "McPherson" discreetly lettered on one side, a doll house reflection of the British preoccupation with tartans inspired by Victoria and Albert who, upon rediscovering the Highlands, upholstered, carpeted, and draped Balmoral with tartans to a fare-thee-well.

Index